WIN CHRIST

How to Get Ahead in the Spiritual Race

RICK S. BELL

Win Christ

ISBN 978-0-578-04682-2

<u>Also by Rick Bell:</u>
The Invisible Pulpit
The Challenge of Faith
Things Unseen
Come Out and Be Separate
The One Who Overcomes:
   Perseverance and Victory in the Book of Revelation

<u>Contact:</u>
ricksbell@yahoo.com
www.bamboobell.blogspot.com

CONTENTS

INTRODUCTION

"DON'T GO away just yet," the host announced as the speaker stepped down. "We have a door prize! Some lucky winner is going to receive ALL of the materials that are outside for sale!"

As he prepared to pick a name from a box, I prepared to leave. I had already sat for more than two hours, and had never really won anything before. Besides, I didn't really wish to clutter my shelves with all of the speaker's books and videos, and there were others in the audience who seemed more interested.

Then I heard him read my name!

After some applause and congratulations, I went home with a big bag full of goods that I didn't really want. Too bad the door prize wasn't a new car!

At home, however, I looked over all the materials and actually ended up using them. It turned out to be a nice win after all! Sometimes we can't fully appreciate the gifts we receive until we make further discovery of them.

The apostle Paul spoke about further discovery of Jesus in terms of "winning" or "gaining" Christ (Philippians 3:8). Many Christians have won Christ in the sense of believing Him for the forgiveness of sins, but have failed to discover what they've really got. There are treasures to be found in a growing relationship with *Him*, and these treasures are often missed- even by religious people. They are easily missed because it can be quite difficult to nurture a relationship with an *invisible* Lord, especially in a day when technology and media stir our senses everywhere we go.

How is one to relate with what cannot be seen? It is much easier to be entertained! There must be a deliberate turning of the heart to what is not seen. That means to give God first place, and esteem everything else as secondary or insignificant by comparison. This is what Paul meant when he said, **I count all things loss for the excellence of the knowledge of Christ Jesus my Lord...I count them as rubbish (Philippians 3:8).**

Though God is invisible, He will manifest Himself spiritually to those who make the effort to believe. **He is a rewarder of those who diligently seek Him (Hebrews 11:6).** He comforts and strengthens those who yield to Him. He reveals that the *unseen* is greater and more powerful than that which is visible.

Things unseen

On a college campus in China, I got into a conversation about the Lord with several Chinese students. It seemed to be going really well, until a girl came along and began to argue with me. She was absolutely closed to any idea that God even exists, and she began to rattle off her objections. I tried my best to deal with her, but as I did, the rest of the group ended up leaving. This was a little unnerving because she had ruined what seemed to be a promising conversation. Now it seemed I was getting nowhere with her and we were just wasting time.

Then it happened! All of a sudden, her entire face changed. She began to radiate a glow, and she completely changed her tune! "Now I understand! Now I understand!" she exclaimed, "God DOES exist, and you came here to tell us about Him!" It was as if heaven had just interrupted our conversation and instantly opened her eyes. It had nothing to do with what I was saying. She had responded to something spiritual for the first time.

It is our response to God, not what we do for God, that makes us truly spiritual. It is not about church attendance, doctrines, and traditions. It is about revelation and responding to God's truth. It is not about gritting teeth and trying to do better. It is about experiencing God's love and being transformed.

God's love is powerful. Many believers miss it, though, being caught in the snares of ignorance. They do not know what they have in Jesus Christ, so they settle for religious 'business as usual.' Paul desired to win Christ, because he knew there was so much more to experience, even though he had already received so much. The same power that turned that persecutor into an apostle is available to all of us.

It is not the "Christian religion" that brings life, but the growing relationship with Jesus Christ Himself. It is not Christianity, but Jesus who is **the way, the truth, and the life (John 14:6).** He does not just point to the heavenly prize- He is the prize itself! **Nor is there salvation in any other: for there is no other name under heaven given among men, by which we must be saved (Acts 4:12).**

Is that fair?

Some have objected that it isn't fair to suggest that salvation can only be found in Jesus, especially when there are so many other religions and philosophies in the world. But it needs to be understood that Jesus did not come to introduce the 'right religion.' God the Father sent Him to die and to take away the sin of the world (John 1:29). God sacrificed His only Son for those who rejected Him- the Just for the unjust. Many religious founders have produced their systems and philosophies, but none have given us their own sons or died for their enemies. It doesn't seem fair that Jesus, the only perfect Man in the sight of God, should die for sinners. Yet He did:

> **All we like sheep have gone astray; we have turned every one to his own way; and the LORD hath laid on Him the iniquity of us all (Isaiah 53:6; KJV).**

Nor has anyone else ever risen from the dead and ascended to God's throne, yet that is where Jesus is now! And He still offers Himself to all. He is waiting to rescue the lost and heal the sick. **Whoever believes in Him should not perish, but have eternal life (John 3:16).**

Have you believed in Him? Those who believe win the greatest Gift they never deserved.

"Do you believe? You will see greater things than these" (John 1:50). He reveals His glory and His love to those who persevere. This is what brings about change and victory in our lives- not rules and regulations.

The prize is before us and the great race of faith lies ahead. In China, they cheer at sporting events by shouting "Jyah Yo! Jyah Yo!" This means, "Add Fuel! Add Fuel!" I hope these chapters may spur you on in the same way, and add fuel to your faith in this day when so much else is competing for our attention.

CHAPTER 1

AMAZING TRUTH

Amazing Grace, how sweet the sound
That saved a wretch like me
I once was lost, but now I'm found
Was blind but now I see

THE HYMN, Amazing Grace, has an amazing story behind it. It was written by John Newton (1725-1807), a ruthless and hate-filled man who drove a ship and sold African slaves. Through many incredible adventures, the Lord eventually got his attention and changed his life through faith in Jesus Christ. After his conversion, he became a very influential preacher in England.

He went from monster to minister! That God should have such mercy on one who was so merciless astounded him. That God could so abundantly love one who was so unlovely brought him to his knees. Why would God do that for him, of all people? Grace was, to John Newton, AMAZING!

It was not a teaching that he simply learned, accepted, and lived with. It was not just a decision he made at one time. It was a wonder that changed his life. It compelled him to worship and serve God exceptionally, and it can affect every believer in the same way.

What could possibly be more amazing than the grace of God? The Lord of glory hung on a cross for undeserving sinners. That includes all of us!

"But I wasn't a slave trader! I was always nice enough to others."

Perhaps, but even if we have been relatively good compared to a slave trader, none of us deserved grace any more than Newton. One sin makes us offensive. Consider this verse that's not quoted very often: **Dead flies putrefy the perfumer's ointment, and cause it to give off a foul odor (Ecclesiastes 10:1).** One drop of ink is all it takes to discolor pure water. One hole is all it takes to render a glass useless, and one sin is all it takes to ruin us. **The wages of sin is death (Romans 6:23).**

Yet it is all too easy to forget this. Our culture winks at sin; no, it even encourages sin. But if sin is viewed in light of the purity and glory of God it will be seen for what it is: ODIOUS.

It is odious and destructive. Temptations deceive and lure unsuspecting souls into traps that end in misery. Sin drives us to hell, as the demons drove the swine off the cliff to drown in the lake below (Luke 8:33). Too often, others suffer for our sins as well.

Besides the damage it does, sin is offensive to a holy God. He is insulted and rebelled against every day. Yet in amazing grace, He cancels and forgets all the sins of those who turn to Jesus.

Like John Newton, many believers start out with amazement that they received such favor and love when they deserved punishment. But it is all too easy to take this for granted and drift into a common mode of Christian living. The wonder eventually subsides and the Christian life becomes business as usual. However, it does not have to be that way.

Keep moving

As one grows spiritually, the amazement should actually *increase*. We know just a little of God's glory now, but one day at His throne it will be abundantly clear. There, they can't help but continually cry out: **"Holy, holy, holy, Lord God Almighty..." (Revelation 4:8).** There we will have perfect vision, but even now vision is possible through His Spirit and the learning of His Truth.

The Christian faith is *spiritual*. It's not about doing your best and trying to be good. It's about power from on high (Luke 24:49)! It's about being filled with the Holy Spirit of God and allowing the life of Jesus to shine through. This is different from simply becoming religious. Before he believed in Jesus, Paul was one of the most religious men on earth. His religious zeal moved him to persecute the early church, until he had a direct encounter with the risen Lord (see Acts 9). After that, everything changed!

John Wesley (1703-1791) was also a very religious man, even a missionary for the cause of Christ. In the beginning, his efforts ended mostly in failure. Yet everything changed for him one day when he heard someone reading about how God changes the heart, and in his own words, "I

felt my heart strangely warmed."[*] That little flame that he caught gradu-
ally increased into a great revival fire!

Whether you get knocked to the ground by a ray of light or whether
you simply take a moment to place trust in Jesus for the forgiveness of
your sins, it is the inward work of the Spirit that makes the difference.
The Spirit will come to those who ask to receive Him (Luke 11:13; Acts
8:15).   It was the power of the Holy Spirit in the book of Acts that
enabled the disciples to come out from hiding and boldly witness to
hostile authorities. It is the Spirit's power that enables us to come out
from a fallen nature and live a godly and overcoming life.

It is the power of the Spirit that works miracles, whether they are personal changes in your life or in the works that you do. If miracles are not
seen right away, do not give up. God is always working, and often the
miracles are unseen. Sometimes faith gets the greater exercise and reward
when it must continue without seeing immediate results. Changes can and
do come instantly, but normally spiritual growth is progressive. It is
through faith *and patience* that we inherit the promises (Hebrews 6:12).

As the Christian faith must be spiritual, it must also be in *truth.* It is
the Truth that sets us free. This however, must be qualified. It is not just
knowing the truth. Many people know the truth and still remain in
bondage. The devil even believes in God, and trembles (James 2:19).

The truth must become personal. This does not mean that truth
changes from person to person. God's truth is absolute and does not
change according to one's preferences.   It means that Scripture is under-

---

[*] See *Journals of John Wesley,* May 24, 1738.

stood in such a way that it speaks directly to the heart, as if God had written it especially for you. The truth is understood in a way that applies personally in your particular situation. This comes through the Holy Spirit as He 'illuminates' God's word. It is exciting when He gives a greater understanding of Jesus through the Scripture- an understanding that touches more deeply than the common understanding of the text. The mistake of many Christians is to settle only with a natural understanding of Biblical truth. They can learn from books, pastors and teachers and certainly be helped, but they've missed the empowerment of receiving their own spiritual revelation.

Paul probably had greater revelation than anybody, and if he had remained content with that, he would still outshine most of us. Yet he had a longing to discover *more*. Paul's experience of truth drew him into a continual pursuit to win Christ. This was so much his desire that he cut himself off from his prestigious standing with the world:

> **I count all things but loss for the excellency of the knowledge of Christ Jesus my Lord: for whom I have suffered the loss of all things, and do count them but dung, that I may win Christ (Philippians 3:8, KJV).**

Paul already knew Jesus intimately, yet he would not stop in the holy pursuit: **I press toward the goal for the prize of the upward call of God in Christ Jesus (Phil. 3:14).** He would not be content with status-quo religion. He would rather suffer for Christ than enjoy all the comforts of the day.

Paul acted on a principle that many today fail to realize: the treasure that we have in knowing God grows richer as we grow closer to Him. As we grow closer to Him, His love shines brighter through us, and sin and temptation become stripped of their powers.

Nice and moral vs. life and love

The pursuit, or the desire for God, marks a healthy Christian faith. This should not be confused with simply being a nice, moral person with good values. One does not have to be a Christian to possess those.

The religious, nice, moral person may know the truths pertaining to God and salvation. He may believe them and try to live his life accordingly to a degree. But there is no FIRE. He sets his own standards as to what is right and wrong. He sings *Amazing Grace*, but is never really amazed. He may do his duty and show up at church on Sundays. He might believe that God has prepared an inheritance for him in heaven, but he daily acts as if nothing has happened. If his team wins the Super Bowl, however, he will be in a good mood all week!

It's great to have your team win the Super Bowl, but it can't compare with the joy of the Lord. Though many don't know it, spiritual joys are far better than what the world has to offer. Yet it is all too easy to substitute worldly joys in place of spiritual. That is like settling for the so-called cheeseburgers we used to eat in China before McDonald's actually came around.

There were, here and there, western restaurant wannabes. They had signs and menus with pictures of decent looking cheeseburgers. Seeing those pictures made the mouth water, but when the time came and they brought the food to the table, it hardly looked anything like a burger! Think of a slab of pork blubber with goat cheese and a fried egg on a sweetened bun, topped with tomato paste. We were desperate, so it had to do.

Many Chinese friends told us they weren't crazy about western food. Go figure! When McDonald's finally came, though, they crowded in droves. And we would never again settle for the pork blubber with goat cheese! In a similar sense, spiritual joy is much greater than what the world has to offer. It takes faith and deliberation to hold out for that which is greater, but this is a difficult task when the heart is so enamored with what is immediately available.

The task can become easier as we grow. Most people do not become Super Christians overnight. Spiritual growth is a process, and it happens as the heart is affected by the knowledge of Jesus. Lots of people have head knowledge while their hearts remain unaffected. Spiritual growth happens when the heart is *drawn.* This is why it is so important to ask the Spirit to bring revelation to the heart.

It is for today

It is very common for Christians to think of spirituality as a matter of "having devotions." We are discussing *a life of devotion.* We are suggesting that it is still possible to be a saint in today's world. It is still possible to do the works of Christ, and even **greater works than these (John 14:12).** There must be no throwing in the towel and saying, "that was for another time." **Jesus Christ is the same yesterday, today and forever (Hebrews 13:8).** Faith presses on like Abraham and says, "I don't care what it looks like or how I feel. God is able to do what He has promised!" (See Romans 4:17-22).

The life of faith becomes supernatural when we invite Jesus in. **"Behold, I stand at the door and knock. If anyone hears my voice and opens the door, I will come in to him, and dine with him, and he with me" (Revelation 3:20).** The problem is that many of His people are not hungry. They are too busy filling up on the imitation joys of the world.

Spiritual hunger does not come unless it is believed that God's truth and ways are more amazing than we already know. With divine revelation of even the basics, we will be drawn like Paul and strive to press on. Nothing else will matter.

"But how can I believe?"

It starts by changing your mind about what is good and what is bad. Agree with God that sin is loathsome, and turn from it all. Be convinced that Jesus is **all together lovely (Song of Solomon 5:16),** whether you feel that yet or not. If the heart is to be changed, the mind must first be changed. It is like making the necessary preparation, as Aaron and his sons had to make careful preparations for the sacrifices they were to offer to God. When an offering was placed on the altar, fire from God came down to consume it. This caused the people to shout and worship (see Leviticus 9:24). When the mind is properly aligned to agree with God and His ways, spiritual fire will eventually fall upon the heart and cause it to shout and worship. If it takes time, don't give up. The ground will eventually thaw if you tend to it long enough. Keep yourself frequently in the Word of God, think on it slowly and prayerfully, and obey whatever you already know to do. It will not be long before the Lord blesses you.

It may be that God will do a great work through you in our day. The denying Peter probably never dreamed he would preach so powerfully at Pentecost. John probably never expected such heavenly visions to come when he was first exiled to Patmos. And Paul probably had no idea that he would influence the entire western world, while suffering persecution after persecution.

An amazing truth is that God can use any of us! Studying the Bible will reveal this and so much more. God will exalt those who approach Him humbly (James 4:10). On the other hand, it is possible to have all the right knowledge and yet be proud as a zealot, 'defending the truth.' There is fire in the Word, and it must be handled carefully.

CHAPTER 2

FIRE IN THE WORD

"SINCE THE BEGINNING of time, mankind has been fascinated with fire!" So began a student in one of the speech classes I had taught in America. She was going to demonstrate how to do an amazing fire breathing trick. I was concerned about safety issues and whether or not this should be allowed in the classroom. Having assured me that there was nothing to fear, and that she had done the trick many times before, I let her continue. This was definitely going to be one of the most unique demonstration speeches in the class! As she dipped two skewers into gasoline, I got a little nervous and hoped that no school officials would be coming down the hall. When she did the trick, the flames went higher than anyone expected. The class cheered, she finished well, and I was happy to give her an A.

The next week, however, she failed to show up to class. "Where is she?" I asked her friend.

The friend replied, "She did that fire breathing trick at a recent party and ended up getting burned."

Thankfully, she eventually recovered. Fire is fascinating indeed, yet it is quite dangerous when it is mishandled. The Word of God is like that as well. **"Is not my word like a fire?" says the LORD (Jeremiah 23:29).**

The Bible is no ordinary book. It contains 66 different books and at least 40 different authors from different times and places, yet it remains consistent in its theme of redemption. Though the official canon was recognized by men, it is a work that no man or group of men could have ever created. It explains the condition of humanity and the world, and provides answers to life's greatest questions. It would be difficult to get just three people to agree on these issues, let alone 40. It also contains verified historical accuracy and a multitude of prophecies that have been fulfilled. Over three hundred Old Testament prophecies concerning the Messiah were fulfilled to a tee in the life of Jesus.[*] It is also miraculous that the Bible has survived all of the attacks against it throughout history. It has been banned and confiscated, ridiculed and burned, and yet it remains the most influential book in the world. You can't put out the fire in the Bible!

Fascination with fire

Moses was fascinated with a fire he saw in a bush: **"I will now turn aside and see this great sight" (Exodus 3:3).** Since the Bible is no ordinary book, it should draw us in the same way. It is often approached, however, as if it were little more than an ordinary bush.

---

[*] See Josh McDowell's *Evidence that Demands a Verdict*.

In our postmodern day, many challenge the Bible and try to reduce it to the status of a human book full of contradictions and errors. They then turn and read the Scriptures as if they are the judges of what is to be accepted or rejected. They assume that they know more than the millions throughout history who have "blindly" trusted the Word and have been changed by it. They take what they believe to be an "enlightened" position and are reluctant to put stock in anything they read. But this does not help them to receive the victory and power that's available for their lives. It is more like a smothering of the flame. And sometimes it is just a cover-up for sin.

"Are you suggesting we just ignore all the problems with the Bible?" No- but have faith! Though many have tried to dispute the authenticity of the Bible, none have ever succeeded in ultimately disproving it. Any supposed contradictions or errors can often be explained satisfactorily. There are books devoted to that, written by wise and intelligent scholars.

There are legitimate difficulties that should not be denied, but there is no reason to get hung up on them. Any actual errors that are found in the Bible (from copyists and translators, for instance) do not affect the main teachings of God. The actual reliability of the copied manuscripts that have been handed down from ancient times is more trustworthy than those of any other ancient literature. It has been remarked that it is nothing short of miraculous that the discrepancies between all the remaining manuscripts are so few.

There are plenty of answers out there for the skeptics. In my experience, however, I have found that it is more often with them a heart problem than a knowledge problem. Skeptics are often unwilling to receive any answer that can resolve their supposed difficulties. No answer is ever good enough. There is an unwillingness to trust the Bible, and then it becomes a matter of pick and choose. They become their own final authority.

The better way is to receive the Word by faith. It is not a blind leap or an unreasonable faith. It is an acknowledgment of a standard- something one can stand on, stand for, and remain standing in the end. It has been tried and proven as such, throughout history and all over the world.

When Moses approached the burning bush, he was told to take off his sandals, **"for the place where you stand is holy ground" (Exodus 3:5).** It doesn't matter whether you read with your shoes on or off, but the same attitude of reverence is needed in order to receive from the Bible. There are spiritual revelations that come forth from the pages of Scripture that will never be had by those who think they are "above" it all.

Getting the fire started

When I first started reading the Bible it seemed to do nothing for me. Here was a book full of life-changing and world-changing truth, and there I was spiritually asleep. I just didn't get it. The fire needed starting from God's Holy Spirit. God's Word is a living Word, but it only lives in us as His Spirit ignites the flame. This eventually happened when I prepared my heart and came like Moses to the burning bush. The Holy Spirit will light the fire if there is patient and prayerful dependence upon Him to bring spiritual revelation out of the passages we read.

After years of Bible reading, I still need the Spirit to fan the flames. Whether it is a familiar passage or a new passage, the reading can always be fresh. There are depths to Scriptures that can be discovered by those who dig into them. This means that concentration is required. The Bible can't be read like a modern novel. It must be thought on and considered. There must be desire for spiritual revelation and deeper understanding. Even scholars well along in years of Bible study can still glean something new from an old passage. But they must come to the Word as students, not experts.

Students of the Word must take care to learn with the heart as well as the mind. It is easier to check the commentary written in our Study-Bible margins than to *take time* and digest the Word for ourselves. Nothing wrong with enjoying the gleanings of others, but we need to get our own gleanings as well.

Here are some ways to get good gleanings (what I am talking about here, is Scriptural meditation):

- Prepare your heart. Be prayerful and expect that the Lord will speak through His Word.

- Spend some time in the passage. Think through each sentence separately. Consider the meanings of individual words. Think on the passage throughout the day, or even the week.

- Read through entire books in the Bible, don't jump around aimlessly. Consider verses within their context as well as on their own.

- Find other related passages or contrasting passages and consider how they might complement each other.

- Try to understand difficult passages, but don't get stuck on them. Move on to what you can work with.

■ Put yourself into the passage and think of the feelings, expectations and experiences that were involved at that time.

■ Think of how it applies to today. Reflect on how it might apply to you personally, or how you might personally apply it.

Don't take fire for granted

My student thought she had it all together and still got burned. Those who get ahead in Scriptural knowledge need to be careful that they do not get away from the main goal, which is to grow closer to God. It is easier to get puffed up with the pride of having learned something than to be truly transformed into the likeness of Christ. It is a natural temptation to desire recognition for what we know, and it often prevails within the Church.

The Pharisees loved to argue with each other. However, they seemed more concerned with their own authority than with the truth. Thus they failed to grow. Some Christians also love to argue the Scriptures- just check the Internet! Is it for love of the truth or for the pride of winning a debate?

Sometimes the truth is ignored simply for convenience. I heard of one seminary student who was studying in his denomination's school. During his studies, he began to question a certain position that they traditionally held. In his research he came up with all kinds of evidence that seemed to prove that position wrong. He took the evidence to the leaders and asked them if there were any ways to answer the challenges, but they had no answers for him. Instead, they simply told him, "This is just what we have always taught, and it is what we have to teach."

Sometimes the stakes are too high to turn around. Sometimes the honest seeking of truth is hindered by blind spots. Other times it is hindered because of pride. Stubbornness happens to even the best of Christians.

Back in the 1700's, two giants of a period known as The Great Awakening fell at odds. John Wesley, the father of the Methodist movement, and George Whitefield, one of the first great itinerant preachers, were close friends and responsible for the conversions of many. They experienced all kinds of revival as the gospel spread like wildfire across England and the American colonies.

Then came the clash. Wesley became disturbed by some of the theology his good friend was teaching. As much as Wesley pleaded and reasoned with him, Whitefield would not change his position. The tension between them increased, and the conflict eventually became public. Wesley preached a fiery sermon denouncing Whitefield's theology. Whitefield then responded by publishing a 31-page pamphlet, denouncing that sermon as "sophistry." Their rivalry went on for a good length of time.

No objective observer could deny the godly character in the lives of *either* of these men. It would also be hard to overlook the fruits of their ministries. Yet the fire of theological controversy burned the two.

Danger in dogma

There are tenets of the faith that should not be compromised. Cults play with fire because they take Scriptures out of context and use them to manipulate their followers.   It is difficult to convince them of their error because they are spiritually blinded.

Bible-believing Christians may not be spiritually blinded, but they often have blind spots. They can end up placing too much importance on side issues or traditions and become unable to fellowship with anyone who might have a different perspective.

Once in China I was ordering a bowl of Over-the-Bridge Noodles. This consists of a bowl of tasty broth that noodles are added to, along with thin slices of raw meats and vegetables. They get cooked instantly as you dump them into the steaming broth. The man was asking me what I wanted to put into my particular bowl.

"Do you want peppers?"

I said, "Yes," and in the peppers went.

"Chicken meat?"

"Yes." And in the chicken meat went.

It was going well enough, until he said, "Do you want pork fat?"

I said, "No," but there went the pork fat, straight into my bowl! Then he pointed to the pickled celery.

"Do you want this?"

I said, "No," but in went the pickled celery!

"Do you want the sweet vinegar?"

"No." Now I had sweet vinegar. It was obvious that we were not communicating.

Sometimes people get so STUCK in their thinking that they cannot hear anything but what they want to hear. This was the Pharisees' problem when they rejected *The Truth* that stood and spoke right in their very midst.

When William Carey, 'the father of modern missions,' first presented a sufficient argument to go to the nations with the gospel, his elder said, "Young man, sit down. When God pleases to convert the heathen, He will do it without your aid or mine." This elder was not listening to anything but his own cherished notions.

What may not be well known about this elder, Dr. John Ryland, is that later he actually *did* support the cause of world missions. Dr. Ryland humbled himself, changed his position, and did what was right. He is an excellent Christian example. How many are willing to admit it when they are wrong?

Many fail to ever change. They have too much at stake. They have championed their cause, they have built their reputations, and they have written their books.

That said, there is another excellent example found for us in Wesley and Whitefield. Although neither confessed that they were wrong, John Wesley and George Whitefield eventually agreed to disagree agreeably. After several years of opposition, they once again became friends and respected each other's differences. Neither of them changed their positions, but there were no more hard feelings. Wesley even preached the sermon (upon Whitefield's request) at Whitefield's memorial service. They fulfilled what Paul wrote in **Philippians 2:1-2:**

> **Therefore if there is any consolation in Christ, if any comfort of love, if any fellowship of the Spirit, if any affection and mercy, fulfill my joy by being like-minded, having the same love, being of one accord, of one mind.**

Unity exists among these fruits of true faith, even in the face of doctrinal disagreement. Are there so few today *having consolation in Christ,* comforted from His *love,* enjoying the *fellowship of the Spirit,* and having *any affection and mercy-* that there can be no unity? Instead, we tend to unify over theological systems, denominations, or mission statements. If someone does not hold to this or that crucial side issue they are disdained and pitied as one who is "missing it." Fellow Christians then divide like the tiny Lilliputians in *Gulliver's Travels,* who argued over the issue of whether eggs should be broken at the big end or the little end!

Granted, there are legitimate differences in the church, and sometimes the body of Christ must recognize that it is better not to force an arm to be a foot. If you prefer the big end over the little end, then go to the Church of the Big End. Better to be with others who are like-minded. Let it be done in humility, though, respectfully acknowledging those who differ (like Wesley and Whitefield). Still accept and love the Church of the Little End.

It's the fruit that counts

Good theology is important, but the Bible is not a textbook that God requires us to master in that sense. It is a supernatural book that He wants to use to develop faith and bring fruit in our lives. Without this, any right thinking is still a barren tree. If you are right about every point of theology and still mistreat your family or friends, you are *wrong*. If the spirit is wrong, the tree is rotten.

This does not mean that there shouldn't be any concern for correct theology, but it should be kept in its proper place. We must not worship doctrines but worship God. It is not so much what we know; it is *Who we know and how we know Him*. In some cases it is important to defend the truth, and certain truths are non-negotiable. But not everything is worth debating. It is more important to model Christ and to show God's love.

When doctrines should be discussed, it should be done in love and humility. In good fellowship, the Lord may really bless it. If done as a know-it-all it is bound to be fruitless. Wesley well said, "I dare not speak of 'the deep things of God' in the spirit of a prize-fighter or a stage-player." Our old friend John Newton also had some choice words here:

> "Self-righteousness can feed upon doctrines as well as upon works... Controversies for the most part, are so managed as to indulge rather than to repress this wrong disposition; and therefore, generally speaking, they are productive of little good. They provoke those whom they should convince and puff up those whom they should edify."**

In other words, don't play with fire! Keep humble, seek the truth, and let the fire in the Word become in you a living flame of love.

** *Letters of John Newton, XVII*

CHAPTER 3

ALIENS AND STRANGERS

THE PEOPLE had caught a glimpse of him on the street. More and more gathered toward him to see what was going on. Before long it was a crowd. He entered into a shop and several followed close behind. They all found it so interesting, and speculated with each other about what he might buy. They giggled like children when he actually spoke to them!

After he left, they all huddled together and verbally replayed the details of the exciting event. They would probably remember this for a long time. At least, they would be sure to talk about it that night at home with their families.

No, this wasn't a day in the life of Elvis Presley! This happened to me in China because I was in a place where I stood out so noticeably different from the local people. Unlike the diverse 'melting pot' culture of America, foreigners in rural China get noticed.

It is easy to stand out as a foreigner in a foreign land, but it is not always easy to stand out among our own people. Yet as representatives of

God's kingdom, we are called to stand out: **As He who called you is holy, you also be holy in all your conduct; because it is written, 'Be holy, for I am holy' (1Peter 1:15-16).** The question is: what does it really mean to be holy?

The technical definition of holiness is simply, 'to be set apart.' There should be a definite contrast between believers and the rest of the world. In the midst of so much spiritual confusion and darkness, Christians are called to **walk in the light as He is in the light (1John 1:7).**

This can be a tricky issue. On one side, there are Christians who go to the extreme and act like self-righteous Pharisees. They criticize and condemn all the unrighteousness they can find. They are clearly 'set apart,' but they are sending a wrong message of legalistic religion to those around them. On the other side, there are Christians that don't want to ruffle any feathers, and they blend right in with the culture like everybody else. They rarely make a stand for anything, and often live according to a standard lower than God's.

The answer, as always, is Jesus. Jesus had strict words against unrighteousness, and even cracked a whip at the sinners in the temple. But he also refused to condemn an adulteress, and gladly ate and drank with sinners in their homes. Love for what is right must be balanced with love for those in the wrong, and love for those in the wrong must be balanced with love for what is right.

Please be encouraged to *walk in the light as He is in the light.* Do not be afraid to meet and love people on their own ground. At the same time, however, do not compromise and meet them in sinful environments, or do as they do. It may be politically incorrect to make a stand for something that is right and true, but make it anyway! Let the world know that you dance to a different tune. Be neither intimidated nor snobbish.

Not an option, but a call

I was being nice when I said, "please," in the last paragraph. The truth, however, is that this is our calling, and to live otherwise reveals a bad condition. The apostle John wrote,

> **If we say that we have fellowship with Him, and walk in darkness, we lie, and do not practice the truth: But if we walk in the light, as He is in the light, we have fellowship one with another, and the blood of Jesus Christ His Son cleanses us from all sin (1John 1:6-7).**

It is a terrible mistake to think you know Jesus when you do not care to walk in His ways. Rather, there is cause for alarm, **for if you live according to the flesh, you will die (Romans 8:13).**

Such verses were not written to threaten us with fire and brimstone, but to show us the better way of abundant life. Sadly, many people in our culture will not receive any kind of statement that may challenge their way of living. They will instead be offended like little babies, not understanding that their best interest may be at heart. There will also be objections, like…

"Isn't the gospel about freedom?" Yes. It is about the freedom to be holy and to receive the blessings of God.

"Aren't we saved by faith alone?" Yes, but genuine faith results in change.

"Weren't the Corinthians accepted as carnal?" Yes, but great pains were taken to correct them.

Why desire less than the best? Contrary to what the world says, holy living is not somber and stuffy. It is right living, and when everything is right, we are usually more at peace. I can still use my computer when it is acting funny or dragging, but I am much happier when it is working the way it was designed to run. God has designed us for holiness, and we will find our lives work better under His design than under our own.

Those who follow the ungodly ways of the world follow the wrong design. **There is a way that seems right to a man, but its end is the way of death (Proverbs 14:12).** Thus it is better to walk in the ways of God and gain life, though in the eyes of many it may appear *strange*.

The best place

Believers need to think of themselves as foreigners, and as heirs to a wonderful kingdom. **Therefore, since we are receiving a kingdom which cannot be shaken, let us have grace, by which we may serve God acceptably with reverence and godly fear (Hebrews 12:28).** There are such privileges that we have as children of the King, yet we act as though we are insignificant and have so little.

At one time, I worked for a prominent company in the business world. The president of this company was well known, a public figure, but I felt like a peon. I thought about the honor it would be if he was ever to recognize me and invite me into his lush office, but chances for a relationship with the big boss were very slim. And he was only the president of a company- how much less a chance to relate with those in high government!

What are they compared to the Almighty Lord of the Universe? I am invited into *His* office every day! He has even entrusted the most important work to me, and has promised to provide for all my needs. Every believer has the same extraordinary privileges, and yet many consider themselves little more than peons. They do not consider **what manner of love the Father has bestowed on us, that we should be called children of God (1John 3:1),** and so they are not motivated.

It is a privilege to be God's child. It is a privilege to be His ambassador (2Corinthians 5:20), and to be a stranger in this land. There is an everlasting inheritance waiting. Why settle for a world that will burn? **Blessed is the man whose strength is in You, whose heart is set on pilgrimage (Psalm 84:5).**

In a strange land

As citizens of heaven, believers will never really quite fit in down here. We live according to a different culture. This is the testimony of the greatest saints: **They admitted that they were aliens and strangers on earth (Hebrews 11:13; NIV).**

The heroes of the faith listed in Hebrews 11 sought a better country. We may not always feel like a 'hero of the faith,' but we can certainly identify with these saints as fellow pilgrims. Peter exhorted us to live as such, to live **as strangers here in reverent fear (1Peter 1:17; NIV).**

The natural tendency is to want to fit in and get most comfortable here, but aliens belong to another world. I stand out in China because I am from America, but the truth is my home is not really in China *or* America. Jesus declared that those given to Him were not of this world even as He was not of this world (John 17:14). Some people might feel awkward about this, but it is actually very encouraging. We have a kingdom to look forward to where *all is well.* We can be happy that our present world with all of its problems is only temporary.

I'll never forget the time we had a layover in Hawaii on our way home from China. We checked into a hotel and I wanted to rest, but I needed to mail something right away. I found my way to the hotel's gift shop. My mission was to see if I could buy any stamps and mail the letter from there. This may sound simple, but I was drowsy, jetlagged and used to living in China.

At that time, my Chinese language was not so good, so I would have to rehearse in my head how I was going to ask for something. Then I always expected the other person to only half understand me and ask me to speak again. Often I would not understand them clearly, either. If I needed change, it wasn't always available; and if I asked directions, they were usually too vague. Things seldom seemed to work very simply at that time in China.

So there I was in a daze, approaching the counter in the gift shop. I remembered that I was in my own culture now and could speak English, so I asked without any problems, "Can I buy stamps here and mail a letter?" Then it seemed amazing to me that the lady understood me perfectly, the first time! And then I understood her as well! She said there was a stamp machine around the corner and that I would need correct change to use it. For a moment I got nervous because I didn't have any change. But that was no problem at all, as she was quite willing to make change for me. I got the coins and then expected to get lost looking for the machine around the corner. But there it was, just like she said! I didn't know if it would really work or if it would eat my money, but I put the coins in and out came the stamps, just like they were supposed to. Then she told me where I could find a mailbox. Everything went off so easily, without a hitch. I was no longer struggling in a foreign culture. I was home!   This was a picture of how things will be in the Kingdom of God. For now, we struggle as we go through this world, but in the Kingdom everything will go smoothly. Many things are wrong in this world, but in the Kingdom everything will be the way it is supposed to be. We will finally be at home.

Not somber, but glad

Being different is a good thing, because **you are a chosen generation, a royal priesthood, a holy nation, His own special people, that you may proclaim the praises of Him who called you out of darkness into His marvelous light (1Peter 2:9).**   Praise is not inspired by rigid religious burdens. Praise flows from the gladness of belonging to God. **You have filled my heart with greater joy than when their grain and new wine abound (Psalm 4:7; NIV).**

"But how do I get glad?" Gladness comes by faith. Faith recalls the fact that all sins have been forgiven. Faith rejoices in the fact that it is not our holiness or unholiness that determines our acceptance level with God. He loves us as if we were perfect- because we were perfected in Christ (Hebrews 10:14). We are not talking about striving to live holy in order to get in good with God. In Jesus, we are already in with God as good as we can get! Believing this should produce thankfulness, and thankfulness is a form of gladness.

Gladness also comes through obedience. **My beloved spoke, and said to me: "Rise up, my love, my fair one, and come away" (Song of Solomon 2:10).** Obedience needs to be seen as a response to love, not as a means to earning it. In this way His commands will not be burdensome (1John 5:3). A heart motivated by love will be more than happy to serve the Lord.

Love is the key, but that does not mean there will always be goose bump feelings. God has demonstrated His love for us in Christ, and that is enough to go on. Sometimes it takes the steps of obedience before the heart actually feels warmed. Sometimes the heart may feel nothing. Feelings should not be the determining factor. We walk according to faith in the truth, and the truth is that God loves us.

Nonetheless, every person needs to experience God's love at some time or another. Every now and then, we need the goose bumps. If the experience of His love seems elusive, it is best to go to the Lord in prayer. That is a holy act in itself. Always keep the lines open with Him. It is helpful to speak honestly to Him and to keep coming back, no matter how often you might fail. He will meet you where you are. Be it ever so little, He will accept what you've got (Luke 21:2-4; 2Corinthians 8:12).

Perilous heights

When you do *rise up* and *come away* from the ways of the world, you are bound to meet with opposition. The devil does not want this. Other believers may not understand. We should be sensitive and try not to alienate other people, but we should not be intimidated. King David was not concerned about what others thought when he danced before the Lord (see 2Samuel 6:14-23). He *undignified* himself before the people, but his heart was on God. When Michal, his 'dignified' wife criticized him, the Lord honored David and punished her. When we really find our acceptance in Jesus, we will think less of how others perceive us.

The devil may try to spoil a higher walk by working hard to bring discouragement. **Resist the devil and he will flee from you (James 4:7).** Do not give in to discouragement, which is often unbelief in disguise. It is easy to dwell on failures and bemoan our shortcomings, as if our works determine our acceptance with God. The better way is to practice faith and rejoice in His mercy.

Helplessness and sense of failure can be our worst tormentors if we are looking to ourselves, or they can be our friends if they remind us to look to Jesus. Turning to Him, we can see His grace that has put up with all our failure, and can trust Him to bring forth *His* holiness instead of our own. As holiness is an act of worship, it is an act of faith: **For we through the Spirit wait for the hope of righteousness by faith (Galatians 5:5).**

It also takes faith to realize that believers are, in a sense, already completely holy in Jesus Christ. It has nothing to do with any accomplishment on our part. It is the great blessing of **Christ in you, the hope of glory (Colossians 1:27).** This is considered more in the next chapter.

Chapter 4

Loosen Up

THE RECIPE calls for two eggs. Can you picture the Three Stooges? Larry, Moe, and Curly immediately throw in two eggs, shells and all! Then the recipe calls for a can of mushrooms. So Larry, Moe, and Curly throw in *the actual can* of mushrooms. A teaspoon of salt, and in goes the spoon with the salt! You can imagine the rest.

That is good comedy, but when it comes to living the Christian life, many believers unwittingly misapply the recipe, and the result is anything but funny. There are many ingredients for holy living found in the Bible, but these ingredients are often misunderstood or wrongly proportioned. The main ingredients of love, grace and faith are often overlooked, and an over-emphasis on rules and works spoils the pot.

Forget about rules and works for a moment and consider that holiness is actually a GIFT that the Lord has *already given*. The Bible says that **if anyone is in Christ, he is a new creation; old things have passed away; behold, all things have become new (2Corinthians 5:17).** That means not just fixed up, but brand spanking new!

There was a great exchange at the cross: for God made Jesus **who knew no sin to be sin for us, that we might become the righteousness of God in Him (vs.21).** We may see ourselves as being way off the mark, but what the Bible says counts, and it declares us to be *the righteousness of God* in Jesus.

Of course, there is an outworking of this in relation to Christian growth, but in one sense the believer is already perfect- as holy as he or she can ever be. It is a result of the Lord's work: **For by one offering He has perfected forever those who are being sanctified (Hebrews 10:14).**

Perfection in Christ

"Brother," you say, "I'm anything but perfect. Just ask my family." This needs to be understood as a spiritual reality, in spite of feelings or what is seen. Spiritually, believers are perfect in Christ. It is the outward working of this that so often falls short, in the mind, the emotions and the flesh.   That's what sanctification is all about- the outworking of the righteousness of God in these areas of our lives. It is about the inward spiritual reality manifesting itself on the outside. This is where so many people seem to have problems.

This outworking of righteousness does not come by formula but by faith. **The righteousness of God is revealed from faith to faith; as it is written, "the just shall live by faith" (Romans 1:17).** Faith in what? That God sees us as already righteous in Jesus. He is our righteousness! **Of him you are in Christ Jesus, who became for us...righteousness and sanctification (1Corinthians 1:30).** It is a gospel blessing to be relieved of the great stress of having to strive after an unobtainable perfection. The relief can come through believing that perfection has already been obtained along with forgiveness in Christ. **Colossians 1:27** speaks of **Christ in you, the hope of glory.** There would be no hope if it depended on works.

Here is where a choice must be made. Do you by faith focus on these wonderful realities and at the same time give thanks to Jesus for covering every sin and failure? Or do you spend more time struggling with weaknesses and a perceived 'sinful nature'* that never seems to get better?

Loosen up, and believe! **For whatever is born of God overcomes the world: and this is the victory that has overcome the world, even our faith (1John 5:3-4).** Don't deny the weaknesses of the flesh, but see the battle already won in Jesus. Then, from this position of victory, you are ready to resist sin and temptation.

For if you live according to the flesh you will die; but if by the Spirit you put to death the deeds of the body, you will live (Romans 8:13). By the flesh, you cannot conquer the flesh. You might become self-righteous, or fall into despair because of all the setbacks. On the other hand, by the Spirit of the gospel, resting in the love of Jesus, there is power to really put away sin. The experience of His love makes it easier to resist temptation. It is like the experience of taking a shower: no one wants to roll around in the mud after they've just been cleaned.

---

* The term, 'sinful nature' originated with the NIV Bible. It is an unfortunate translation of the Greek word for 'flesh.'

I am not suggesting that there won't be any more struggles. We don't just take one shower and then forget about it. Faith needs to be exercised throughout life, continually coming back to the love and acceptance that is ours in Jesus. As it is written, the righteousness of God is revealed **from faith to faith (Romans 1:17).**

The mind must continually be renewed by the truths of the gospel, and be ready at all times to reject the lies and accusations that Satan will bring. "You'll never be good enough! You blew it again! How can God love you?" Then the conscience will join in: "You're not making any progress! Your sins are deeper than you can ever make good!" Thoughts like these may come, but they don't have to stay.

Rather, in the Spirit of the gospel, reject such lies and say to them, "If I listened to you, I would be denying all that Jesus purchased for me on the cross! Thank you Jesus for your amazing grace! You are my righteousness!" **For freedom did Christ set us free: stand fast therefore, and be not entangled again in a yoke of bondage (Galatians 5:1; ASV).**

No woe

Romans 7 has been a controversial subject throughout church history. The chapter records a great struggle in the mind of Paul, who confesses that the good he wishes to do does not get done, and the evil he wishes to avoid is what actually comes forth. He confesses that he is **carnal, sold unto sin (vs.14)** and lets out a great cry, **"O wretched man that I am! Who will deliver me from this body of death?" (vs.24).** It might all be summed up in the proverbial cry, "WOE IS ME!"

This is controversial because there are some who believe that Paul was only describing his life before his conversion to Jesus Christ. Others argue that this is Paul as a believer, revealing every believer's inward struggle. There are good arguments for both sides of the debate.

For either case, the answer is found in **verse 25:**

I thank God- through Jesus Christ our Lord.

No matter how imperfect a Christian sees him or herself, and no matter how impossible it may seem to improve, it is unbelief to remain in the state of "woe is me" as expressed in Romans 7. Paul acknowledged the struggles of the mind and the flesh under the law, but he moved on to thanksgiving in the light of the gospel.

Does this mean it is wrong if we can relate to those struggles mentioned above? No, but to be blinded by them and to remain in them is wrong. Christians who get down on themselves in these struggles are operating under a sense of the law. Because of the gospel, God loves us and accepts us in spite of our sins. We have become dead to the law that we may be married to another- Jesus (Romans 7:4).

No matter how vast the depths of sin appear to be, it is unbelief to dwell on them. The law condemns such depths, but you are no longer under the law. You may agree that you are a terrible case concerning the things you do and don't do, but in Christ the woe is gone!

I thank God- through Jesus Christ our Lord. Don't forget to move on to Romans 8. **There is therefore now no condemnation to those who are in Christ Jesus (8:1).**

This doesn't mean that struggles with the flesh are completely over, but it does mean there is RELIEF in what Christ has done. And that sense of freedom will loosen you up to do better than all the threats of the law ever could.

The proper place of works

James wrote, **"be doers of the word, and not hearers only, deceiving yourselves" (James 1:22).** Obedience or lack of obedience is a good indicator of where one's heart truly is. Failure to put forth any effort to obey God's word reveals a heart deceived. It has not yet truly understood what God has done, and has failed to respond to His grace.

An enlightened heart will discover that doing God's will is to receive food that others know nothing about (see John 4:32-34). It will desire to work out its **salvation with fear and trembling (Philippians 2:12)-** not the cringing kind of fear and trembling that doesn't know it's acceptance with God, but an awestruck sense that **it is God who works in you both to will and to do for His good pleasure (vs.13).** Christ in you, the hope of glory!

Many people take this for granted. They do not stop to consider themselves as vessels of God. Lacking faith, they either:

1. Take no care to live holy at all, or,
2. They try too hard to be good on their own.

This is where the church needs fear and trembling- fear and trembling that we fall into neither of these two traps. Instead, there is need to be aware of the truths of God's grace, presence, and power.

Sanctification is not the result of what we do, but of what we believe. Be **confident of this very thing, that He who has begun a good work in you will complete it until the day of Jesus Christ (Philippians 1:6),** but faith must be exercised.

The great and fundamental sin

Charles Finney taught, "The great and fundamental sin, which is at the foundation of all other sin, is unbelief. The first thing is, to give that up - to believe the word of God." He was right, but it's not always easy. The father of a demon possessed boy was honest with Jesus when he cried, **"I believe; help thou mine unbelief!" (Mark. 9:24; KJV).** He said this with tears, obviously anxious before the Lord.

Thankfully for him and for us, the Lord does not always depend on our complete confidence in order for Him to work. But we make things much harder on ourselves when we fail to exercise faith. The Bible teacher, Arthur Pink expressed it like this:

> "Oh! It is unbelief, failure to rest upon the exceeding great and precious promises of our God, and forgetfulness that He is ever by our side, that makes our feet leaden and causes us to drag along so wearily."

The better way is to **trust in the LORD with all your heart; and lean not on your own understanding (Proverbs 3:5).** Trusting in the Lord, Peter got out of a boat and walked on water (Matthew 14:28-31), but he began to sink as he focused on the wind that was raging all around him.

It may not be wind that we are focusing on, but our own understanding and unbelief. That can sink us just the same. The sense of difficulties and hopeless-looking circumstances can overwhelm like a storm. No apparent change in sight! *But lean not unto your own understanding.* Jesus is here. **In all your ways acknowledge Him, and He shall direct your paths (3:6).**

Our Great and Fundamental Friend

The trust should be in Jesus Christ as *a person.* That may sound obvious, but it is easy to get distracted and trust more in a concept, theology, or historical facts rather than in the actual living person of Jesus Christ. We do not have personal relationships with data, history, or theological systems.

"I have called you friends" (John 15:15). Friends who hang out together tend to become more like each other. They also trust each other. Friends of Jesus must trust Him for their righteousness, but they must also be trustworthy to Him to do their part.

Make no mistake- even though it is God who brings spiritual growth, we can't just remain passive. There is still need to be yielded to Him and to do what we know to do. A relationship is a two way street. Blessings don't just drop out of the sky, while ignoring what His Word says to do. That's not the way it works. Jesus must be Lord as well as Friend. That means doing what He says, and doing it willingly.

Some think that submitting to His Lordship is a hard business, but that is actually where peace can be found. It is has been proven that young children feel more secure when their parents have proper boundaries for their behavior. Believers learn that the Lord's boundaries and directions are reasonable and for their best interests. Even His discipline **yields the peaceable fruit of righteousness to those who have been trained by it (Hebrews 12:11).**

The Law was a hard schoolmaster (Galatians 3:24-25), but the Lord is our Friend. We serve because we love Him and agree with Him that His ways are best. Serving Him is an act of worship. According to the law we will always fall short, but we are not under the law, we are **under grace (Romans 6:14).** We are **accepted in the Beloved (Ephesians 1:6).**

If Jesus hadn't paid it all, there would be reason to be tense. Because of the cross and the resurrection, the tension between God and us is gone. Now we may **serve him without fear (Luke 1:74).** Those at rest are more workable, and they work more efficiently. A good musician plays better when relaxed than when nervous and tense. The same goes for living holy in the sight of God and man. It can be done without being overly self-conscious and uptight.

CHAPTER 5

THE TRUTH ABOUT DEATH

LONG BEFORE I became a Christian, I had at least some sense of the seriousness of death and the afterlife. Strangely, my friends were different. One day the radio was on, and a song from a group called The Grateful Dead started to play. Their lyrics caught my attention. The singer was boasting, "I may be going to hell in a hand basket, baby, but at least I'm enjoying the ride!"

I said to my friends, "Isn't this song idiotic? I mean, the guy knows he's going to hell- and he's glad about it? That is nuts!" I thought I was delivering some profound wisdom there but my friends just stared at me like I was the nut.

The band, AC/DC had a similar song. This was "Highway to Hell," in which the singer declared there were "no stop signs, speed limits, nobody's gonna slow me down." Nobody did. He died of alcohol poisoning not long after recording that album. Did the band stop to think about this after they lost their friend? They took on a new vocalist, and recorded the hit, "Hell's Bells" only five months later.

Hard rock music thrives on a fascination with death and hell. Blood and guts are spilled out all over our film and television screens. Video games allow us to murder and die without any consequences. All of this takes place with little (if any) consideration that **it is appointed for men to die once, but after this the judgment (Hebrews 9:27).**

There are spiritual forces at work, trying to keep down any thoughts that might arise and consider the serious transition from this life to the next. This is one reason there is so much noise and distraction in our culture. Everywhere we go, we are bombarded with sensory stimulation, whether it is blaring music or gaudy advertising displays. People's schedules become so overloaded that there is little time for contemplation of what they are sowing for the rest of eternity. **For we must all appear before the judgment seat of Christ, that each one may receive the things done in the body, according to what he has done, whether good or bad (2Corinthians 5:10).**

Many people take great care to eat right and to keep their bodies fit, and yet do nothing to insure the well being of their souls! Jesus is the only answer, **nor is there salvation in any other: for there is no other name under heaven given among men, by which we must be saved (Acts 4:12).** Yet the gospel is often cast aside as if it were an item on a menu.

Preparation is not a big concern; or if it is a concern, many wrong paths are taken. It would be nice to fit in with the Politically Correct and say, "it doesn't matter what you believe or do," but that would be contrary to God's Word. It would also make life seem pretty irrelevant. What we believe and do really counts! We are sowing for the ages to come.

Because of Jesus, there is no need to fear. He died and rose again, that we might have hope. It is true that **the soul who sins shall die (Ezekiel 18:4).** But, **"he who believes in Me has everlasting life" (John 6:47).** This is good news! The truth about death is that it can be a transition into *life.*

Dead *and* alive

Faith in Jesus brings eternal life. Yet eternal life is not just something reserved for a far off time after we die. It is something that can be experienced now. Jesus said, **"I have come that they may have life, and that they may have it more abundantly" (John 10:10).** Many Christians fail to enjoy abundant life now, though, because they have not identified with Christ in His death.

How shall we who died to sin live any longer in it? Or do you not know that as many of us as were baptized into Christ Jesus were baptized into His death? (Romans 6:2-3). Believers cannot just "add Jesus" to their lives. They must be born again (see John 3). They must consider themselves dead to sin and alive to God (Romans 6:11). Temptations may feel strong, but they might be countered by believing the truth: "that was for the old sin-loving me, but that old me is dead. I died to that with Jesus."

Paul experienced great victory in spite of his difficult life. The reason for this is because he considered himself **crucified with Christ (Galatians 2:20).** In Philippians chapter 3, Paul revealed the secret of living in His power:

That I may know Him, and the power of His resurrection, and the fellowship of His sufferings, being conformed to His death; if by any means I may attain to the resurrection of the dead (vs.10,11).

He understood that victory was found in knowing *Him and the power of the resurrection;* but in order to know resurrection power, something must first die. Now this is not necessarily as gloomy as it may first appear. What did Paul mean by being "conformed to His death"? I do not think he envisioned putting on black and looking for his personal demise. Rather, he wanted to be obedient to God's will, even as Jesus **humbled Himself, and became obedient to the point of death, even the death of the cross (Philippians 2:8).** It seemed Paul wanted nothing less than to be as obedient as Christ. And so he wished to be conformed to His death - to be able to say, **"Not my will but Yours be done" (Luke 22:42).**

You have heard the expression, "what goes up must come down." Here we might change it to, "what goes down must come up." Jesus humbled himself unto death, and God raised Him up from the grave. That is life-giving power, and that same power works toward us who believe (Ephesians 1:19). What we lay down for the Lord comes back up in some greater way or another. There is life to be had in dying.

Responding to the call

Then said Jesus unto His disciples, "If any man will come after me, let him deny himself, and take up his cross, and follow me. For whosoever will save his life shall lose it: and whosoever will lose his life for my sake shall find it" (Matthew 16:24-25).

Notice that phrase, *"If any man will come after me…"* This is not talking about the casual churchgoer who has made a decision for Christ at one time or another. It is referring to those who diligently *come after* God, like the Shulamite woman pursues her lover in the Song of Solomon.

In chapter 5 of the Song, the lover is knocking at the woman's door, but at first she will not get up to let him in. She has already gone to bed: **"I have taken off my robe- how can I put it on again? I have washed my feet- how can I defile them?" (vs.3).** At this point, she is more concerned with herself, and she pursues him *not*. But she has a change of heart, and soon gets up to let him in (vs.6).

To her dismay, she finds him gone. She then longs for him and begins her search through the city. Now she has denied herself - she is out of bed and "coming after him." As she describes him to her friends, it is not just a physical description, but a romantic soliloquy expressing her heart's desire. (see vs.10-16).

Not for the timid

The Lord said we must take up the cross. The Shulamite woman experienced pain and humiliation when she began looking for her groom. The watchmen of the city found her, beat and bruised her, and even took away her cloak (Song 5:7). This could have been avoided had she stayed in bed! It was a consequence of her pursuit. Living for Jesus involves suffering for His name. **Yes, and all who desire to live godly in Christ Jesus will suffer persecution (2Timothy 3:12).** This means you may take some heat at school or work, maybe even within your own home. There may even be greater challenges in the anti-Christian days ahead.

It is here that many people say, "Thanks! That may be good for you. See you later!" They would love the Savior but would rather not take on any hardships that might come from living for the Lord. But they are nearsighted. They miss the greater benefits that come as a result. **Blessed are you when men hate you, and when they exclude you, and revile you, and cast out your name as evil, for the Son of Man's sake. Rejoice in that day and leap for joy! For indeed your reward is great in heaven (Luke 6:22-23).**

There is a place of high honor and reward for those who take flack for Christ. **For this is commendable, if because of conscience toward God one endures grief, suffering wrongfully. For what credit is it if, when you are beaten for your faults, you take it patiently? But when you do good and suffer, if you take it patiently, this is commendable before God (1Peter 2:19-20).** He already loves us, but this seems to imply that He takes a special pleasure for those in such circumstances.

It must also be remembered that suffering can happen whether one follows Christ or not, but the Lord's people have a special promise: **that all things work together for good to those who love God, to those who are the called according to His purpose (Romans 8:28).** This is not true for those who don't love God, and shouldn't be used as blanket words of comfort for every bad situation. But for those who love God, it means that even our trials and tribulations, difficult as they may be, will result in a greater good: **For I consider that the sufferings of this present time are not worthy to be compared with the glory which shall be revealed in us (Rom.8:18).**

Society promotes happiness at all costs. If we are in pain, we quickly grab for the pain relievers. Comfort is good, and by all means do not unnecessarily wallow in pain if there is a legitimate way to relieve it! Do not forget, however, that there are hidden blessings in trials.

In fact, we are told to rejoice in our sufferings: **count it all joy when you fall into various trials; knowing that the testing of your faith produces patience (James 1:2-3).** Paul said that **we glory in tribulations (Rom.5:3).** The psalmist said, **"It is good for me that I have been afflicted; that I may learn your statutes" (Psalm 119:71).** As gold is refined in the fire, so God can bring about a greater good through suffering.

Do not make the mistake, though, of thinking that God wants you to suffer, or that He is the One bringing it all upon you. It is the devil who comes to steal, kill, and destroy, while Jesus came **that they may have life, and that they may have it more abundantly (John 10:10).** It is true that God brought severe punishments to His people under the old covenant, but under the new covenant Jesus took all of our punishment and removed the curse of the law. It is true that God disciplines His children (Hebrews 12:5-13), but there is a difference between discipline and child abuse. It would be a strange discipline for a father to give his child a terminal illness, yet some have taught that God would do just that in order to "teach us a lesson" and somehow be glorified by making us miserable. Not so! They forget that there is a devil in this world and that suffering often comes straight from him. Suffering also comes because people are sinful, and they make wrong choices. And bad things happen sometimes due to the simple fact that this is a fallen world. No, God is not the problem. He is the answer! **Let no one say when he is tempted, "I am tempted by God" (James 1:13).** But God will **make the way of escape, that you may be able to bear it (1Corinthians 10:13).**

The Shulamite woman suffered pain and humiliation from the city watchmen. Yet it did not seem to faze her. It was her lover she was looking to, and this *enabled her* to endure the beatings. The same can enable us in whatever we are going through. She did not even give her pains a second thought. Her message to her friends was: **"If you find my beloved, that you tell him..."**

Tell him what?

That "he should avenge me"?

That "I am faint from the beatings"?

That "I can't take it anymore"?

No. The message was, **"That you tell him I am lovesick" (Song 5:8)!**

This had quite a profound effect on her friends. Though she was bruised, they acknowledged her beauty (6:1), and were themselves drawn to her lover! The beauty of Jesus shines through to others when they see what we, in love, go through for Him.

This is the wonder of the cross. While it is a stench and offense to some, it can produce a beauty that attracts man to God. **Unless a grain of wheat falls into the ground and dies, it remains alone: but if it dies, it produces much grain (John 12:24).** Just as a greater good came from Jesus dying, so will more fruit be produced in our lives when we lay down our own agendas for His. And so Jesus bids, *"follow Me."*

Resist the devil

The enemy also seeks followers and has many tricky schemes. He will be happy to provide alternative routes and mislead even the best of saints. He must be RESISTED.

When Jesus spoke of His death, and Peter said it should never happen, Jesus recognized this as a temptation from the devil. **"Get behind me, Satan! You are an offense to me; for you are not mindful of the things of God, but the things of men" (Matthew 16:23).** In rebuking Peter, Jesus faithfully resisted.

It was probably quite tempting, though, to hear the words, *"This shall never happen to you!"* Jesus might have been so relieved. The burden would be removed; He and His disciples could devise another plan. After all, He was in very nature God, and He certainly didn't deserve to die. His disciples were loyal, and they would surely back Him up in any decision He made. By men's standards it sounded so right. But Jesus resisted, and stayed fixed on God's purposes. Thank God He did!

And so we are to do the same, though it can sometimes mean a harder route to go. Like Paul, and like the Shulamite woman, it is necessary to keep the proper object and desire in view, so that there is willing endurance. This was one of the keys to Jesus' victory:

> **...who for the joy that was set before Him endured the cross, despising the shame, and has set down at the right hand of the throne of God (Hebrews 12:2).**

What was the joy that was set before Him? Besides the joy of seeing the reconciliation of the world to Himself, there was the joy of doing and completing the Father's will. Jesus said, **"My food is to do the will of Him who sent me, and to finish His work" (John 4:34).** This is the food that would ultimately satisfy. **Isaiah 55:2** quotes God saying, **"Listen, listen to me, and eat what is good, and your soul will delight in the richest of fare" (NIV).**

We need not settle for junk food. There is far better in store when submitting to God. We feast not on bread but on the Bread of Life. Proper nourishment keeps us healthy and alive.

Death is an enemy, but it need not be feared. It has lost its sting! (1Corinthians 15:26,55). The truth about death is that Jesus triumphed over it. Whether it is working through present trials, or at the end of our lives, it can be a gateway to peace and glory.

CHAPTER 6

PEACE AND GLORY

I HAVE BEEN involved in Chinese missionary work that has extended all the way to the borders of Vietnam, Laos and Burma. At one time I actually went into Burma, although I had to do it secretly.

I was helping Chinese Christians set up a farm project inside the Burmese border. They were allowed to come and go without any trouble from the government, but an American like me would be out of the question. The brothers assured me that if we bypassed the official checkpoint and took an alternative road through the mountains, I would be able to go in and no one would ever notice. Being very much tied to the project, it seemed I should at least visit the site, and after prayer I had an assurance that it would be alright- this time.

We went through the scariest mountain roads I have ever been on! For two hours I drove up and down steep narrow paths, bounced along rocky terrain, and wound around sharp curves, with drop offs to the side. I had really started to doubt my previous assurance!

Once we got to the actual site, all was well. I felt safe being there, but dreaded the thought of having to drive back on those roads after a couple of days.

In the middle of the night before we were to leave, I was awakened by the whistling of a loud boisterous wind. The bamboo housing began to shake and rattle violently. Nervously, I gathered some of my things together to put them in my bag, fearing that they might get blown away with the roof of the hut! After several minutes of this, an idea came to mind. I sat up and spoke to that wind just like Jesus: "Peace! Be still!" And it stopped, just like that! All was calm.

A few minutes later I heard raindrops, and they just got heavier and heavier. The rain began to pound, and I began to worry about the drive back in the morning. It was hard enough on the dirt roads, but it would be even worse in the mud. Maybe even impossible. So in like manner I spoke to the rain: "In the name of Jesus, stop raining!" But this time, nothing happened. Perhaps the rain was hard of hearing! I commanded it to stop, but it only got worse.

It stormed the rest of the night and did not let up until morning. During that time I went through all kinds of panic-filled thoughts: "What if I can't leave and someone catches me here? What if it continues to rain for several days? What if the only way out is through the checkpoint? What will they do to me there?" I hardly slept at all with my stomach in knots. The worse part of it was that I knew I should be trusting God and resting in Him, but I found it nearly impossible to be at peace with the storm.

That morning the rain turned to a light drizzle, and we decided to leave a little bit later in the day. It was a muddy ride and at times we had to just inch around the steep curves. The 4-wheel drive got us through some extra slippery spots. In the end we made it, all shook up, but none-theless well.

Because everything worked out fine in the end, I am able to relate that story with peace and calm. It was the uncertainty in the bamboo shack that had me all worked up. If I had known for sure that we would get back home safely, I could have slept quite comfortably through the storm.

Peace in the certainty

Jesus slept comfortably through a storm. It was the disciples who woke Him, saying, **"Master, Master, we are perishing!" (Luke 8:24).** Jesus calmed the wind and the waves and then responded to the disciples, saying, **"Where is your faith?" (vs.25).**

Strange question! Didn't they have faith in going to Jesus? Weren't they supposed to show faith by asking Him to take care of all of their problems? That is how many often view faith, but that is not the kind of faith that keeps them calm in a storm.

This is Biblical faith: **the substance of things hoped for, the evidence of things not seen (Hebrews 11:1).** The disciples showed no evidence of any hope in reaching the shore. If they had believed, they would not have cried out that they were perishing. They could have remained calm by considering that no storm could overtake Jesus whether asleep or awake. Their safe arrival was as sure as God exists, and He was there in the boat! Perhaps they knew this, but they were not exercising faith or giving evidence of it at that moment.

There is great peace to be had in the Christian life, knowing and be-lieving that Jesus is in the boat. The peace is forfeited, though, when more attention is placed on the winds and the rain. It may be hard to grasp at times, but the truth is that whatever you may go through, it cannot overtake God or His love for you. Though trials come, they will pass, and though the rains may be strong, He will be able to help you navigate safely through them. **The LORD shall preserve you from all evil; He shall preserve your soul. The LORD shall preserve your going out and your coming in from this time forth, and even forevermore (Psalm 121:7-8).** Since the immediate future is so often uncertain, we have to rest on the certainty of His Word.

I failed to fully rest on that certainty in Burma, but I am growing. The disciples missed it in the very same boat with Jesus, but they grew. Peter was able to sleep soundly in prison the night before he was supposed to be executed (Acts 12:6). If you have missed it somewhere, you can grow too.

There is great peace in the gospel because we have a certainty of our acceptance with God. This is in spite of the fact that there is still so much growing to do. I used to stumble over this, thinking I had to be instantly perfect in all the Christian ideals. I would brood over all the garbage still found in my heart. I understood grace but still beat myself up for the faults I kept discovering. I have learned rather to focus on the certainties of the gospel. Instead of getting self-absorbed and discouraged, I have learned how to simply *give thanks.* The amazing truth is that in spite of all the garbage that surfaces in the heart, **there is therefore now no condemnation to those who are in Christ Jesus (Romans 8:1).** According-ing to His Word, it is a certainty that God is not keeping records of our sin (see Isaiah 43:25, 44:22; Jeremiah 31:34; Hebrews 8:12, 10:17).

The law was *against us,* demanding payment for every sin, and Jesus Christ paid the bill! The check was enormous and our pockets were empty, but **the kindness and love of God our Savior toward man appeared, not by works of righteousness which we have done, but according to His mercy He saved us (Titus 3:4-5).**

The law condemns sin, but we are under a different law now that is actually working *for us:* **For the law of the Spirit of life in Christ Jesus has made me free from the law of sin and death (Romans 8:2).** Though sin may continue to pop up in the Christian life, though death may come, they count for *nothing* in the long run. They are like an opposing team that may continue to make goals, but the points never register on the scoreboard. The score has already been settled. No "woe is me," but, **"thanks be to God, who gives us the victory through our Lord Jesus Christ" (1Corinthians 15:57)!**

Perfection and peace

"But I am not getting any better!"

Are you sure you are not getting any better? Growth occurs over time and often is not noticed while it is happening. And sometimes God works secretly in areas of our lives while we happen to be focusing elsewhere.

"But I fail Him so much!"

Nonetheless, He is looking at you through Jesus, and **He has made us accepted in the Beloved (Ephesians 1:6).**

Think of how misled they were before the Reformation- fearing purgatory and buying indulgences, doing penance and making pilgrimages! The gospel is not about self-abasement, becoming a monk or doing better. The gospel is GOOD NEWS!

Here is the good news: we need not wait until everything is perfect to enjoy peace with God. For being justified by faith:

> **We have peace with God through our Lord Jesus Christ:**
> **through whom also we have access by faith into this grace**
> **in which we stand, and rejoice in hope of the glory of God**
> **(Romans 5:1-2).**

We have peace with God. How could any unholy thing have peace with the *Holy One?* Who can say, **"I have made my heart clean/ I am pure from my sin?" (Proverbs 20:9).** Yet One was, and it is through Him that we enjoy such a privilege. He did all the work and we have reaped the benefits.

Peace comes through faith, not works. Otherwise, the holy requirements are too high. One wrong move or one false thought is all it takes to remove any sense of comfort. A sense of failure is bad enough, but fear of God's displeasure is even worse. Instead of having abiding peace, it can feel more like a yo-yo going up and down depending on how well one is doing. This is not only detrimental to peace, but it is sin, because it shows unbelief regarding the work of Christ. Jesus said of the work, **"It is finished" (John 19:30)**, and failure to rest in Him is like saying, "I disagree, there is more that needs to be done."

The just shall live by faith

It is faith that pleases God (Hebrews 11:6), but faith also pleases us! It is faith that brings the peace, believing that God is not angry any more. This is not a passive faith in which a concept (like His love) is simply known and understood. It must be active, a conscious decision to believe and receive it personally.

At one time, I believed and would give my life for the doctrine of justification by faith, but I was not *appropriating it.* I was not living in that grace. Unwittingly, I was trying to earn my acceptance with God. I realized this one day, when eating at a fast food joint. I saw a disheveled looking man in an overcoat walk in. He seemed to have a scowl on his face. I thought, "Is this guy in his right mind, or are we going to make the front page headlines?" Random shootings are too often heard of these days.

I knew this really wasn't a threat, but it did get me thinking hypothetically about sudden death. I had always envisioned a special time of really giving myself to prayer and preparing to die. But now, I thought, what if I was to go without any warning? Would I be ready to face God? In my mind I said yes, intellectually knowing the teaching of God's grace, but in my heart I sensed a trembling. Deep down, I was not ready; I still had more 'good' things to do, and even more 'bad' things to overcome. I needed more time! I passively believed but had not actively received God's gift of acceptance- justification through faith.

It is natural to want to work for salvation, feeling the need to earn God's love. Active faith means rejecting this natural tendency and finding rest in God's finished work. This means one believes he is saved and loved even in spite of his miserable failures. They may come like the wind and the rain at times, but he will **have joy and peace in believing (Romans 15:13),** knowing the certainty of God's grace through the finished work of Christ.

Active faith consciously receives God's gift of grace, not just at conversion, but also in every moment of failure. It is too easy to make the mistake of compartmentalizing grace, thinking of it only in terms of initial conversion, but God's grace is powerful and working everyday. Jesus saves not just at first, but through every storm and failure, all the way to the very end:

> **Wherefore He is able also to save them to the uttermost that come unto God by Him, seeing He ever lives to make intercession for them (Hebrews 7:25).**

That one-time shedding of blood did not only wash away previous sins, but it continues to wash away all sins from here on. This is truly amazing grace. It really is the gift that keeps on giving!

> **Blessed are they whose iniquities are forgiven, and whose sins are covered. Blessed is the man to whom the Lord will not reckon sin (Romans 4:7-8; ASV).**

That is the blessing of peace with God. The sin that we sorrow over cannot foil the power of His grace; and if anyone sees this as a license to sin, they really do not understand or know what it is to be blessed by this grace (also, see comments by Paul in Romans 6:15-18).

Glory, glory, hallelujah!

Having peace, **we rejoice in the hope of the glory of God (Rom. 5:2).** The hope of God's glory brings about effective change because it changes the heart. Condemnation, on the other hand, produces guilt. Guilt tries to work from the outside in, but God's glory changes from the inside out.

God works through conviction, not condemnation. The heart that hopes in God's glory begins to see sin for what it is, and willingly turns from it. Conviction may come with tears, but it is not the same as the burden of guilt. It is more of a release. It results in joy. Active faith will reject guilt, and find refuge in the cleansing blood of Jesus. Then when He appears, **you also will appear with Him in glory (Colossians 3:4).** Not shame, but GLORY!

Everyone desires glory, but few really know what it is. Is it the spectacle of fireworks lighting up the sky? Is it the grand slam home run that breaks the tie in the bottom of the ninth? Is it the shot that falls through the hoop from the other side of the court? These might astound us, but they can't compare to divine glory. The greatest joy and perfection found on earth is only a hint of the heavenly glory that is to be revealed.

Divine glory caused Moses' face to shine so much that people could not handle it. Isaiah saw the Lord's glory and cried, "Woe is me, for I am undone!" Ezekiel and John fell on their faces as if dead. Every knee in heaven and on earth and under the earth will bow before Him and confess that Jesus Christ is Lord (Philippians 2:10-11)! The glory of Jesus will outshine the brightness of the sun (Revelation 21:23). And **you also will appear with Him in glory (Colossians 3:4).** Wow!

We can barely scratch the surface of understanding the glory of God that is yet to be revealed, but we can rejoice in it. We have more than all the world can possibly offer. What did we do to deserve it? Nothing! In fact we deserved punishment and the pits, but being *justified by faith, we have peace with God through our Lord Jesus Christ, through whom also we have access by faith into this grace in which we stand, and rejoice in hope of the glory of God.*

Hallelujah!

CHAPTER 7

PEACE AND LOVE

FILMS AND TELEVISION often present couples 'in love' in nonrealistic ways. Sometimes it just takes a single glance and someone declares, "It's love." Sometimes two people are thrown together into a difficult situation, so 'falling in love' becomes inevitable. Often two characters have hardly gotten to know each other before a passionate first kiss. And too often the newfound 'lovers' end up jumping in bed together.

Popular music also spreads the wrong ideas. The 'love' song is often nothing more than a 'lust' song that promotes passion over relationships. Continual hearing of this music can condition its listeners to equate love with codependency. They then begin to think they must have a successful romance, or else they are hopeless and lost in this life.

Some readers are probably now thinking I sound a bit prudish and should be sent back to earlier times. But I speak this way because I believe there is BETTER LOVE to be had. The devil has cheated multitudes with these false notions of love, and many of them have ended up in despair because of it.

Divorce is at an all time high because couples blindly go into marriage not realizing that they have a genuine misunderstanding of true love. They do not realize that romantic feelings come and go, and as soon as the romance fades they panic and fear that maybe they are not in love any more. They do not realize that there is something greater that comes from the commitment to work through problems together, and to persevere.

False notions of love can also take a toll on one's self esteem. Self-worth is frequently measured by whether or not one is accepted by the opposite sex. The hero is not a hero without a girl swooning all over him. The singer will die if she does not get her man! When one notices all the skimpy clothing of the day, it is obvious that people are desperate for attention. They want to cash in and be 'desirable' but they are putting their funds in the wrong bank! They are more likely to get in trouble than in love. Love must not be equated with sensuality. The feelings from sensuality do not last, and they often lead to heartache.

But God demonstrates His own love toward us, in that while we were still sinners, Christ died for us (Romans 5:8).

Our self-worth is not to be measured by another's acceptance of us- it is to be measured by the death of Jesus Christ upon the cross.

Who on earth has shown love that comes anywhere near equal to the love of Jesus? **Greater love has no one than this, than to lay down one's life for his friends (John 15:13).** The godly died for the ungodly, the just for the unjust, the rich for the poor. His love never fails. It leads to a life in eternal glory. What on earth could equal that?

Jesus knows us better than we know ourselves, and He STILL loves us and calls us His friends! We do not have to pretend to be someone we're not, around Him.

His love is not mushy greeting card stuff, although many people only see it that way. In truth, it is powerful and profound. The secret to living a devoted or consecrated life to God is getting in touch with this incredible love. Paul prayed,

> **That He would grant you, according to the riches of His glory, to be strengthened with might by His Spirit in the inner man; that Christ may dwell in your hearts by faith; that you, being rooted and grounded in love, may be able to comprehend with all saints what is the width and length, and depth and height; and to know the love of Christ, which passes knowledge, that you may be filled with all the fullness of God (Ephesians 3:16-19).**

When the Holy Spirit strengthens the inner man, there is power to see past the deceptive temptations of the world and there is power to resist sin. There is also power to love others. It was the power of God's love that moved me to want to go and serve in China. Before, I had heard guilt producing sermons on why I should go to the mission field, but they did little more than make me open to the idea. I never wanted to, nor thought I would go to China. Then the Lord started to drop hints that He wanted me there. It made me nervous at first, but one day in prayer I sensed such a powerful flow of love coming from His Spirit, that I couldn't help but say, "I'll go anywhere you want, Lord!"

The Spirit will come and strengthen the inner man, but the profound experiences are not the norm. Believers should actually sense the love of

God from time to time, but if there are no goose bumps it shouldn't matter. Feelings are sometimes unreliable. God's love is received by faith.

Love and faith

By faith the heart first receives Christ, but that is not enough. He must *dwell* in the heart by faith as well (Ephesians 3:17). It is possible to receive Christ, and fail to give Him any other thought until the next church gathering. Or sometimes thought is given to Him in the morning and then completely forgotten throughout the day.

In both cases there is a need to believe in God's love, and that it is personal towards us. God's love towards us produces a desire for Him. **We love Him, because He first loved us (1John 4:19).** There are widths, lengths, depths, and heights to be enjoyed. It becomes a life pursuit to be filled to the measure of all the fullness of God.

Jude 21 says to **keep yourselves in the love of God.** This means to convince yourself and always remind yourself of His love. This is not an abstract truth about God, it is a divine reality- God REALLY loves you. Faith is necessary for taking that statement and saying it like this: "God really loves ME." It is not just that God "tolerates me." He "really, really loves me!"

One reason there is so much backsliding and failure in the church is because this love is not really believed. There is great unrest in many souls because they still think that God accepts them, but hardly likes them. The devil does all he can to keep them from finding freedom in God's gospel love. Believers need to resist the unbelief he throws our way.

Take Jesus' yoke

God especially delights in Jesus, and Jesus has invited us *to take His yoke* (Matthew 11:29). One dictionary definition of a yoke is: "a clamp that embraces two parts to hold or unite them in position." Jesus invites us to embrace Him, and offers to unite us into His position.

What is His position with the Father? He is the Father's beloved Son. The Father said to Jesus, **"You are my beloved Son, in you I am well pleased" (Luke 3:22).** The Father is with Him, and He always does those things that please Him (John 8:29). We are invited to join with Jesus in this standing. His position with the Father is transferred to us. So many struggle for acceptance with God, while all along Jesus is saying, "here, take it!" We *do not* always do those things that please God, but He is not taking OUR yoke, we are taking HIS.

Then Jesus says, **"Learn of me" (Matthew 11:29).** Study the One who is perfect; He is our example. He has life to offer, and is Himself the Life (John 10:10; 14:6). See how He has compassion on the multitudes, heals the sick and feeds the hungry. He has the Father's love, *the best love,* and He does not hoard it to Himself, but freely shares: **I have declared to them Your name, and will declare it, that the love with which You loved Me may be in them, and I in them (John 17:26).** So we should do as He does. And we can, being yoked to Jesus. That brings peace, and where there's peace there's joy. No one wants to contain joy. What better way to vent it out than loving one another?

Love produces

Someone once told me, "You can start a chain reaction of love. Do something nice for someone and it might affect their whole day. They will be more inclined to do something nice for someone else, and so on..." Yes, that sounds corny, but it is true that we become encouraged when we receive acts of kindness. The Bible says, **"let us consider how we may spur one another on toward love and good deeds" (Hebrews 10:24; NIV).**

When we sense that we are loved it seems that nothing can bring us down. We in turn naturally show love to others. The problem arises when we lack faith. Forgetting that there is no condemnation causes peace to exit. Or, we become judgmental of others and forget our own failures and the great love that covers all sins. Forgetting grace, love becomes much harder (if not impossible) to convey.

Active faith will claim the peace that is found in Christ and rest in His yoke. Then comes the freedom to love. There is no need to be bogged down with unholy concerns about whether we are good enough or whether we are pleasing to God. These issues have already been resolved. We have but one debt, **the continuing debt to love one another (Rom. 13:8; NIV).** And even though we are already set free from the law, we are told that **he who loves another has fulfilled the law (Rom. 13:8).**

The concern for holiness is proper and right, but the concern to practice love should take top priority. **Galatians 5:6** speaks of what counts: **faith working through love.** This is what fulfills the goal of holiness: **Love will cover a multitude of sins (1Peter 4:8).**

For, you brethren, have been called to liberty, only do not use liberty as an opportunity for the flesh, but through love serve one another (Gal.5:13). If Christians placed servant-type love above quarreling and debating, the world might be won all the quicker. Grace and harmony are much more attractive than legalism and disunity. In addition, a church can get so caught up in its organizational affairs and a primary focus on teaching that it forgets to go out there and love.

Jesus said, **"A new commandment I give unto you, that you love one another; as I have loved you, that you also love one another. By this all will know that you are my disciples, if you have love for one another" (John 13:34-35).** If a Christian is not concerned with becoming holy, something is wrong. Yet, this verse reveals that it is not how holy one is that witnesses to the world, but it is in love for others. Greatness in the church should not be measured by how far one goes in leadership, or who has the most spiritual gifts. **Whoever desires to become great among you, let him be your servant (Matthew 20:26).**

The enemy does not want to see this happen. He likes all the posturing, disunity, and discord. He knows that love is a powerful weapon that overcomes evil, so he will do whatever he can to interfere. He will be quick to point out the unlovely characteristics of others. He will encourage selfishness. He will lie about God and others. Stand fast, watch and pray.

Chapter 8

Peace and Quiet

IT WAS THE SUMMER of 1853. The drought caused great concern throughout the town. The heat and dry weather had practically scorched the pastures. A few more days of this and the cattle would certainly die. It looked absolutely grim for the harvest.

Sunday came along, and the people gathered together for church. There wasn't a cloud in the sky. Then Charles G. Finney stepped into the pulpit and prayed a prayer that one of his associates could remember even twenty-three years later!

Finney prayed, "We do not presume to dictate to You what is best for us, yet You invite us to come to You as children to a father, and tell You all our wants. We want rain! Our pastures are dry. The cattle are lowing, and wandering about in search of water. Even the little squirrels in the woods are suffering for lack of it. Unless You give us rain our cattle must die, for we shall have no hay for them in winter; and our harvest will come to nought. O Lord, send us rain! And send it NOW! Although to us there is no sign of it, it is an easy thing for You to do. Send it now, Lord, for Christ's sake!" There was a hearty, "Amen!" from all in the place, and then the service went on.

By the time Finney got half way through his sermon, the rain began to come down in torrents! His associate recalled, "We could scarcely hear him preach!" Finney then stopped to have everyone praise God for the rain, and gave out this hymn:

When all Thy mercies, O my God,
My rising soul surveys,
Transported with the view, I'm lost
In wonder, love and praise.

"We all sang," said his associate, "at least all hearts did, but many could not for weeping."[*]

There is mighty power in prayer. It is no less than God's own power, and He has put it into our praying hands! Believers who do not pray are missing out on the wonders of actually affecting the universe through the wielding of the highest power to be had.

"But it doesn't work that way for me! I've never made it rain!" Perhaps, but that does not mean that you never will. Prayer contains such untold power that it would be foolish to write it off just because of apparent failure. How long did it take before mankind harnessed the power of electricity? Prayer is something that must be learned. "Lord, teach us to pray!" is the cry of all God's disciples.

---

[*] From *The Reminiscences of Rev. Charles G. Finney,* Remarks of Rev. Joseph Adams, 1876.

History and experience reveals that God works when His people pray. Time and time again, great works or movements were birthed out of fervent prayer.

Charles Finney saw revivals everywhere he went. The first thing he did when entering a new town was to gather those who could pray and get them praying for the meetings. At Pentecost, it is written that the disciples *continued with one accord in prayer and supplication* before that awesome day when the Holy Spirit came like a rushing mighty wind (Acts 1:14). James confirms that **the effective fervent prayer of a righteous man avails much (James 5:16).** What power we forfeit in our lives, when we fail to pray.

Quiet time, power time

"To be a Christian you must have a quiet time every day!"

Not necessarily true. If that is the reason you are going to pray, you miss the point. Rather, it is a good idea to have such a time every day, so that you can keep the spiritual fires burning in your heart, and also equip yourself against trials and attacks of the enemy.

It is a good idea to continue in set apart times of prayer in order to enjoy God's special presence. He is always with you, but there is something special about consecrated time. **"Be still, and know that I am God,"** He says in **Psalm 46:10, "I will be exalted among the nations, I will be exalted in the earth."** It is during this time of quiet, that our relationship with Him is nurtured (*know that I am God*) and that our prayers will effect change in the world (*I will be exalted*). Many do not realize the potential that can result from set apart times with God, and so these times are neglected.

Prayer is a supernatural act for supernatural people. It is helpful to consider the differences between living in the natural world and living in the world of prayer:

NATURAL WORLD	WORLD OF PRAYER
▶ Science and technology perform the miracles	▶ God performs the miracles
▶ Convenience is Lord	▶ Jesus Christ is Lord
▶ Everyone is busy	▶ We remain still before Him
▶ Various entertainments compete to stir our senses	▶ Our senses are stirred by His presence
▶ The hectic pace of the world brings tension and frantic struggles to stay on top of mounting situations	▶ The patient pace of prayer brings rest as we commit our lives to God's tender care
▶ Marketing puts before us everything we 'need,' books and magazines tout solutions to every problem	▶ He supplies all of our needs according to His riches in glory

The problem today is that many Christians live primarily in the 'natural world' and only occasionally visit the 'world of prayer.' Prayer is seen more as a duty to be fit somewhere into the daily schedule. It is often cast aside due to the strains of the day. We say, "I am too tired," or "I don't have enough time to pray." The natural world has effectively triumphed over the spiritual!

The way of victory is to find life in the world of prayer, and carry it over as we step into every natural world situation. **Pray without ceasing (1Thessalonians 5:17)** - this implies that it is possible to be in a spirit of prayer at all times. If the heart is kept in a prayerful state, it will be easier to set apart special times to get alone with God. When actual fellowship with the Lord takes place, prayer will seem less like a duty and more like the privilege that it really is. Prayer brings action. Prayer brings relief. It ushers in a special intimacy with God. When this happens, prayer gets exciting. It becomes all we want: **My soul longs, yes, even faints for the courts of the Lord: my heart and my flesh cry out for the living God (Psalm 84:2).** This is the place of treasure in prayer that is often forfeited by the expediency of the day. There are other responsibilities calling, and our attention spans are short. We give up too easily and buckle under what seems to be the hard work of prayer.

Excitement in prayer

In his famous diary, the early American missionary David Brainerd wrote,

> "Oh! One hour with God infinitely exceeds all the pleasures and delights of this lower world."

How many Christians can say that today? Brainerd found the treasure, and all else dimmed by comparison. Is Jesus any less excellent today? Not at all! Yet we are not always enthralled by His excellence in prayer. Perhaps it may not be realistic to expect every session of prayer to be glorious; Brainerd himself cried out at times to a seemingly distant Lord. But at least we can realize *the potential* that is there and set our hearts to strive for it.

Praying brings in a direct encounter with God, and that should never be dull. Do we get tired and fall asleep? Even the disciples did that; but it is doubtful that we, on that great day when we meet God face to face, will feel like sleeping! Even now prayer has the potential to be just as exciting, but since we do not see Him face to face, faith is necessary.

There is often little exercise of faith in the prayer chamber. Looking more to reason, logic, and the ways of the world can cause our spiritual muscles to become flabby. Believing God answers prayers, we still tend to look for conceivable solutions, forgetting that God likes to work with the impossible. We believe God can change us, but feel that some things require time. That may be true, and that may be how God chooses to work, but why cancel out the possibility of His instant touch, or instant healing? We have not because we ask not (James 4:2).

"Maybe God worked that way in the old days," objects one, or "maybe He works that way with others, but not with me." We need to remember just Who it is that we pray to, and what He can do. Nothing is impossible with God. He **is able to do exceedingly abundantly above all that we ask or think (Ephesians 3:20).**

William Carey, 'the father of modern missions' was an uneducated shoe cobbler who became a Professor of Languages, founded numerous schools and translated the Scriptures into 36 dialects. One of his battle cries was, "We must expect great things from God, and attempt great things for God." Of course, expecting requires faith.

Great expectations

In the past, I realized that there was little of any 'expecting element' in my prayers. It was more or less something of a 'hit or miss' attitude. Maybe God would answer this one, or perhaps I did not pray that one correctly. It was like firing shots in the dark and hoping to hit the right target. Wait and see and hope that God answers the prayer; and if He doesn't, count the loss and hold your head up high. There is not much faith in that.

In order to be able to expect great things from God, prayer must be accompanied by faith in at least these four aspects:

1. Faith that God has heard
2. Faith that God wants to answer
3. Faith that God has the power to answer; and
4. Faith that God *will* answer.

1. Faith that God has heard. It is true that sin interferes with prayer: **If I regard iniquity in my heart, the Lord will not hear me (Psalm 66:18),** but it is not true that you have to be 100 percent pure in order for God to hear you. The despised publican beat his breast in the temple and prayed, **"God be merciful to me, a sinner" (Luke 18:13),** and he was heard. Cornelius was a centurion and not yet a Christian, but his prayers came up as **a memorial before God (Acts 10:4).** It is Jesus who has made a way for us to approach God, and we come before **a throne of grace (Hebrews 4:16).**

If you think you need to be perfect for your praying to be heard, you are not praying in gospel faith. Jesus has you covered. Do not regard iniquity in your heart- that means do not cherish any sin, but do not make the mistake of thinking that any awareness of sin in your life will cancel out your prayers. Let such awareness propel you into thanksgiving to Jesus.

Then ask according to God's will. Prayer out of wrong motives is bound to be ineffective. **You ask and do not receive, because you ask amiss, that you may spend it on your pleasures (James 4:3).** Obviously, God is not going to hear any prayers that go against His Word. You cannot ask to have another man's wife, for example. On the other hand, if you pray according to God's Word, know for sure that you have been heard. And then have:

2. Faith that God wants to answer. Though it may not always be spoken, I suspect many believers feel too insignificant that God should want to honor their requests or bless them. More than once I have heard that there are "too many more important things for God to concentrate on right now. How can I bother Him with my personal needs?" Perhaps there is an acknowledgment of God's greatness in these thoughts, but they mostly represent a lack of faith. There is a failure to trust in God's love and failure to believe that He cares. The Bible says to cast **all your care upon him, for He cares for you (1Peter 5:7).**

The blind man Bartimaeus did not lack faith (see Luke 18:35-42). There he was, begging along the roadside, poor and insignificant, when he heard a great commotion. The crowds were surrounding Jesus, and he heard that "Jesus of Nazareth is passing by!" He called out, "Jesus, Son of David, have mercy on me!" Boy, he had a lot of nerve! Didn't the crowd intimidate him? Why bother the celebrated Man and His procession? It would certainly appear that this Jesus was far too important to be concerned with a lowly beggar at this particular moment.

Some tried to rebuke the beggar, telling him to be quiet. That could have reinforced any hesitation he might have had. But instead, he cried out all the more to Jesus: *"Son of David, have mercy on me!"*

Then Jesus stopped, and ordered that this man be brought to Him. What would happen now? Bartimaeus had disrupted everything! Now he would hear a thing or two and be put back in his place. Instead Jesus asked, "What do you want me to do for you?"

Bartimaeus did not say, "I'm sorry Lord, I see that you are busy. I have distracted you." He didn't even politely say, "Could I bother you for just a minute?" No, he blurted out, "Lord, I want to see!" and Jesus healed him right there, commending him for his faith.

What was his faith? Had someone given him a gospel presentation right there? Did he make a 'decision for Christ' at that moment? His faith was in the goodness, mercy, and power of Jesus. When all else suggested he shrink back, he pressed forward in boldness, believing that Christ would heal.

If a lowly beggar had faith that Jesus would bless, then we who are God's children should be all the more confident. It will be more joyful going to our knees, believing that He is for us and not against us, and that He wants to answer our prayers.

In Matthew 8, a leper asked the Lord if He was willing to make him clean. Those words, *"I am willing,"* must have been the sweetest sound to his ears. The Lord wants to answer our prayers. **He who did not spare His own Son, but delivered Him up for us all, how shall He not with Him also freely give us all things? (Romans 8:32).**

He invites us: **"Ask, and it shall be given you; seek and ye shall find; knock, and it shall be opened unto you"** (Matthew 7:7; KJV). Why would He invite us if He did not want to answer? He loves us more than any earthly father loves his own children. **"If you then, being evil, know how to give good gifts to your children, how much more will your Father who is in heaven give good things to those who ask Him!"** **(7:11).** He desires to do something with our prayers. It was His idea to begin with! And being confident that He has heard, and desires to answer, we must then have:

3. Faith that God has the power to answer. This is elementary. He is God. He is the same God who divided the Red Sea, making a way of escape for the children of Israel. He is the same God who brought water out from the rock. He is the Author of life, and He raises the dead. **With God all things are possible (Mark 10:27).** There is really not much more that needs to be added to that. It is the next one, though, that people usually find difficult. That is, having:

4. Faith that God WILL answer. Will God always give us what we ask for? Consider **John 15:7:**

> **If you abide in me, and my words abide in you, you shall ask what you desire, and it shall be done for you.**

Here is where some hard questions come in. "Why wasn't this prayer answered?" or "How can we know if it is God's will?" There are not always easy answers. Yet this is the very heart of the prayer of faith. The prayer of faith does not bring forth a "yes, no, or maybe" answer. The answer is always, "YES." **For all the promises of God in Him are Yes, and in Him Amen, to the glory of God through us (2Corinthians 1:20).** The prayer of faith considers it as good as done. **Whoever does not doubt in his heart, but believes that those things he says will be done, he will have whatever he says. Therefore I say to you, whatever things you ask when you pray, believe that you receive them, and you will have them (Mark 11:23-24).**

To pray, "if it be your will" is not a prayer of faith if the Bible already reveals it as God's will. It would be ridiculous to pray, "Lord, if it be your will, help me break free from pornography!" Instead it should go something like this, "Lord, you have commanded us not to lust, so now give me the power to resist. Thank you for the power of Jesus to break that bondage in my life. I receive it now in Jesus' name."

So many people need healing. So many have prayed, "Lord, if it be your will, heal this person." I have also prayed that way in the past, but that is not praying in faith. **Matthew 8:17** tells us that Jesus **Himself took our infirmities and bore our sicknesses.** He healed **all kinds of sicknesses and disease among the people (Matt. 4:23)** and He healed **all who were oppressed by the devil (Acts 10:38).** He told the leper He was willing, and His will is also expressed in **3 John 2: Beloved, I wish above all things that thou mayest prosper and be in health, even as thy soul prospers (KJV).**

It is God's will to heal. It is His will to sanctify the body as well as the soul and spirit (1Thessalonians 5:23). A prayer of faith would be,

"Thank you Lord that you bore it all for us on the cross, and that by your **stripes we are healed (Isaiah 53:5).** Bring strength and relief now because of all you have done, in the name of Jesus."

Nonetheless, there is still the question of "what about when this doesn't seem to work?"

When it seems that prayer has not worked, there could be a number of reasons. It could be because of unbelief, but not necessarily. It could be wrong belief (such as, "maybe God is punishing me through this," when He isn't). It could be due to spiritual warfare. It could require certain steps of action to be taken, or it could require waiting and perseverance. Some prayers take time to manifest and require a faithful patience (Hebrews 6:12). It would take up too much space here to go into all of that, and even then there would still be unresolved questions. It is important, though, that such questions and/or disappointments not cancel out our faith in God's promises. **Let God be true but every man a liar (Romans 3:4).**

We may not be blessed to realize the promise at times, but this does not mean we should give up on it altogether. Though the answer does not immediately come forth, it doesn't mean that the dialogue is finished.

The continuing dialogue

> **If you abide in me, and my words abide in you, you shall ask what you desire, and it shall be done for you (John 15:7).**

Jesus has already left us His words. We must know them in order to benefit from them. This is why it is so important to become an expert in the Bible. We want to know what we have so we can use it.

Then we can engage in a continual dialogue with Him. By this I do not mean continual chatter. The dialogue takes place when we present Him with something (*ask what you desire*) and He responds (*it shall be done*).

It may take time and continued believing before an answer is finally realized, but keep expecting the answer to come. Our worship, prayers and supplications should not be sent up in a 'hit or miss' attitude, but in a watchful and trusting expectation that *a difference has been made*. That is a part of the dialogue- our waiting and trusting. A dialogue is not complete if it is only one-sided. Imagine a conversation in which a friend suggests and asks several things to another, and never waits for a response.

In situations where there is no clear revelation of God's will, and no Scriptural promises on which to base any expectations, it may be that the Lord will withhold what we ask for, or shut certain doors. Many of my prayers had failed only to later discover that it was a true blessing that they did. Better things happened or worse things were avoided.

That being said, it is possible to miss out on great blessings if prayer is given up prematurely. Remember John Newton? It was through the faithful prayers of a friend and her family that his miserable life was preserved through numerous trials and reckless escapades. Through the years his sins increased. Surely he appeared to be a lost cause. He even had a reputation as such, but this family never gave up. For years they stood in the gap for this 'lost cause,' and the Lord answered their prayers, eventually turning Newton into a mighty man of God.

Get ready for prayer

It has been said that the best way to learn how to pray is to just keep doing it, but here are some suggestions: Take time to really meditate on Who it is that you are talking to before making requests. Pray in the Spirit (Jude 20). Be conscious not to fall into a rut of speaking religious words meaninglessly or by habit. This includes mindlessly overusing the Lord's name. Pray from the heart. Be honest with God, but don't fall into the trap of grumbling and complaining. If your situation is desperate, try to concentrate more on God's greatness and ability to handle it. Give thanks and praise.

Prayer doesn't always come easy. Ask the Holy Spirit to assist. Be patient, determined and ready. Whoever is serious about growing in prayer can count on opposition. An old English Puritan, Richard Sibbes once said,

> "When we go to God by prayer, the devil knows we go to fetch strength against him, and therefore he opposes us all he can."

The devil would rather keep us in a stagnant, powerless position because prayer has a way of thwarting his works. It is a source of victory and strength. It can also be a source of joy. While it is the Christian's duty, it need not be a chore. The wise Christian knows of the treasure that can be found in prayer, and seeks it.

CHAPTER 9

HOPE IN THE MIDDLE OF IT ALL

THEY WERE WITHOUT HOPE. The Chinese couple's son had been hit by a motorcycle and pronounced brain dead by the local doctors. The doctors told them that they could take their boy home and let him starve to death or leave him at the hospital and the staff would take care of it there.

The parents were not about to just leave their child, so they brought him home and grieved. It was not long, though, before some Christian friends came to the parents and spoke to them. "There is a God in heaven who can heal your son," they said. "Can we pray for him?"

As strange as this sounded, the parents had nothing to lose by consenting. So the friends laid their hands on the boy who had been laying motionless, and they began to pray.

As they were praying, the boy suddenly sat up! He had not responded to anything before that prayer. It wasn't yet a complete healing, but it certainly had begun. *Now* there was hope. And as the days went on, the boy got better and better- thanks be to God!

What would life be like without hope?   Yet so many people plod through their trials as if they will never change. Some people even enjoy wallowing in their hopelessness.

I once walked into a guitar store in a remote part of China. The boys working the store had colored hair and wore spiked bracelets. The music of an old heavy metal group, Metallica, was blaring. I wondered how it was that *their music* had made it to this obscure place? Then the boys started laughing about me, because I was some kind of 'square' foreigner.

I surprised them when I told them, "I used to like this kind of music, and even played lead guitar in a band." Now they were listening! "But I don't like this kind of music any more."

"Why not?" asked one. He seemed sincerely interested.

"Because these guys just sing about anger and frustration, for the most part. They dwell on all the problems but they don't have any answers. There is no hope in their music."

He then responded and asked me, "Well, where can you find hope?" Of course, I was very glad he asked.   I was able to give Him a Bible and we became friends. He was the only one, though. The others in the store were content to keep wallowing in Metallica.

Christians can unknowingly weaken their faith by filling their minds with hopelessness. If it is not depressing music, it may be too much attention to the news. It may happen by reading the wrong books or seeing the wrong films. The world continually pumps out reasons to fall into despair. On the other hand, the Bible is filled with **exceedingly great**

and precious promises (2Peter 1:4) that we can use to rise above all things. Our God is the **God of hope (Romans 15:13).** The choice must be made- get nervous with all the doomsayers, or shut them out and believe God's Word.

No situation is too difficult for the Lord. The situation may be bad, but not cause for panic. We do not need to move to the hills or store up food supplies in fear. **Behold, the eye of the LORD is on those who fear Him, on those who hope in His mercy, to deliver their soul from death, and to keep them alive in famine (Psalm 33:18-19).** Even when there is great reason for the nations to give way to fear and distress, the Lord says, **"lift up your heads, because your redemption draws near" (Luke 21:28).** While the world panics, God's people have opportunities to shine.

Hope vs. hope

The Bible teaches a special hope. We are not talking about hope as in "I hope it doesn't rain today!" We are talking about hope as an **anchor of the soul, both sure and steadfast (Hebrews 6:19),** a security in times of chaos or confusion. As the pilgrim is faced with many trials in a world not his own, so hope keeps him resolute. Hope maintains an eternal certainty in the midst of temporary uncertainty. Biblical hope sees the future belonging to God.

The church is temporarily nearsighted: **For now we see in a mirror, dimly, but then face to face. Now I know in part, but then I shall know just as I also am known." (1Corinthians 13:12).** This is enough vision to get by for now, but it can also be increased. While physical vision naturally seems to deteriorate with age, spiritual vision can become sharper and sharper as we grow in our relationship with God.

One day the clouds that have blocked our understanding will dissipate in the light of God's glorious presence. At that point, all questions will yield to wonder and awe. We will be surrounded by perfect love, and we too will be glorified! **When Christ, who is our life appears, then you also shall appear with Him in glory (Colossians 3:4).**

It's 5:00!

Is the church truly looking forward to this? My fault has been in looking to other items to stir my heart. When I worked for a certain company, my hope was in the clock striking five. Or it was in the hour I could get away to read a good book. Many people place their hope in a more comfortable living arrangement, or the day they can afford one. And how many look forward to the ending of a particular problem, placing hope in its eventual resolution? Not that these are wrong, but such hopes are often disproportioned because we are too nearsighted. We look forward in the TEMPORAL more than the ETERNAL.

Peter wrote in his first epistle:

> **Therefore gird up the loins of your mind, be sober, and rest your hope fully upon the grace that is to be brought to you at the revelation of Jesus Christ (1:13).**

This is a call to do away with lesser thoughts. The mind wanders about too freely, wasting so many thoughts and weakening faith in the process. It is often more drawn to the recalling of a recently enjoyed film than the meditation of the glory of God. There is a war for our minds, which is why Peter said to prepare them for action.

The discipline of self-control is needed that we might cast **down imaginations, and every high thing that exalteth itself against the knowledge of God, and [bring] into captivity every thought to the obedience of Christ (2Cor.10:5; KJV).**

Is this easy to do? Hardly, but soldiers do not become soldiers by wishing they knew how to fight. They go through rigorous training and discipline until the desired end becomes their second nature. The battle for the mind is constant, so it takes the discipline and watchfulness of a good soldier.

The enemy does not want Christians gaining joy from heavenly think-ing. This would draw them closer to God and farther from the attractions of the world. It would diminish the enemy's supply of seductions. The word to believers is: **Do not be conformed to this world, but be trans-formed by the renewing of your mind (Romans 12:2).**

Many are concerned about what they eat. They want to maintain a good healthy body. In the same way, there should be concern for a good healthy mind. The mind is fed all the time, but few think about what it is really eating.   What predominately occupies the mind? Here is the test regarding mind intake: is it CONforming, or TRANSforming?

"Be transformed..." Rather than looking to 5:00, it is better to look to what is eternal, and fill the mind with the thoughts of a greater hope, even the blessed hope:

**...looking for that blessed hope, and the glorious appear-
ing of the great God and our Saviour Jesus Christ (Titus
2:13; KJV).**

**For the Lord Himself shall descend from heaven with a
shout, with the voice of the archangel, and with the trump
of God: and the dead in Christ shall rise first: Then we
which are alive and remain shall be caught up together
with them in the clouds, to meet the Lord in the air: and
so shall we ever be with the Lord. Wherefore comfort one
another with these words (1Thessalonians 4:16-18; KJV).**

Anticipation

When I was a teenager, I used to get very excited about going to rock
concerts. I would wait in line for hours to buy a ticket to see a big name.
Once I had that ticket, my heart was set in anticipation for the show. I
would often pull out the ticket just to remind myself of the big event, and
counted each passing day as one day closer to the show.

Now the coming of Christ will be infinitely greater than anything that
anybody could possibly anticipate on earth. It is unbelief, and getting
caught up in the day-to-day routine that diminishes any anticipation of His
kingdom return. However, we have our ticket, the Word of God, to
constantly remind us and fuel our hearts in expectation. One does not
need to understand everything in the book of Revelation to be blessed by
its description of the end. Though much of it is enigmatic, everyone can
understand and be encouraged by its portrayal of the victory of Jesus and
the end of evil.

The return of Christ should be the guiding hope of the church. Many churches have become just "business as usual," very settled and operating on a routine basis somewhere in the neighborhood. Of course, churches need to be involved in daily operations. They need to check, though, to see if the cart has not gone before the horse. The blessed hope of our returning Lord and the advance of His kingdom should be the motivating factor in all operations. It should motivate joy. It should motivate a desire to do the work. It should motivate an urgency to share the Gospel. It should motivate worship. It should be the banner over our lives: "The King is coming!"

Some people ask why it is taking so long (see 2 Peter 3), but even now He is here through His people. His Kingdom is in our midst (Luke 17:21), though the kingdoms of this world seem to dominate. But wherever His people do His will, His Kingdom is revealed, and it will continue when all other kingdoms fail. For now, He is still working in this fallen world, and that is its greatest hope.

Sharing the blessing

Compared to believers, people without the Lord have nothing to look forward to. They carry their inward burdens alone, having no God to call upon. There is no promise that all things work together for their good. The meaning of life becomes a mystery, and answers are sought out in all the wrong places, yet God is within reach all along. Hope is available in a simple turning to Jesus. The present day can become more meaningful and the Day of Judgment can be approached without fear. But they need to see and hear that God cares. That is where we come in. We not only have hope, but we can offer it to a lost world. We *must* offer it to a lost world - we are their only hope!

As we possess hope in the middle of it all, so *we are* hope in the middle of it all. We have been left to dwell in this world for a short time to serve as ambassadors for Jesus Christ. The world is on a collision course while we are set for heaven. We have the Answer in the midst of so many questions. How can we keep quiet? We have good news! It is always exciting to share good news with someone, and good news is always exciting to hear. We have the greatest news of all: THERE IS HOPE!

Jesus shall return, coming in the clouds with great power and glory (Mark 13:26). He shall right all wrongs. He shall receive worship from all creation. Every knee will bow before Him. His faithful ones will be received unto glory, while the wicked will be struck with terror. Now is the time to share it with those who are in the dark. Now is the time to point them to Jesus, who is the Light of the world.

Chapter 10

Jesus is the Light of the World

I REMEMBER my days before coming to the Lord, when I lived in darkness. Nightclubs and parties were a part of my regular routine. My friends and I mustered up lots of laughs and camaraderie, but it never got past a surface level, and the satisfaction never lasted. Quite often, it would be followed up by a hangover.

A hangover consisted of physical sickness and spiritual emptiness. Any joy that was experienced was now lost forever, only to exist in a memory. In some cases, there would not even be that!

So many people all over the world know no other comfort than to ease their pains in the atmospheres of darkness. Be it drugs and alcohol, the occult, or hedonism, it is a sad and dark reality that people look for life in such avenues of death. How I thank God for rescuing me. How I thank God for abundant life!

With or without

Shortly after my conversion, I reflected upon my life BC - before Christ. I was amazed. I replayed scenes of the past and marveled at the reality that I was always alone. My life during those times could be characterized as WITHOUT. I had been running around aimlessly in the dark. Things that I once thought were meaningful now seemed to be superficial.

After I turned my life over to Jesus, everything changed. Now, I was WITH. His presence in my life brought such sweet companionship that I could not believe I had lived so long *without*. He was with me in every-thing, and leading me in the knowledge of His truth. Today it is the same, although it may often be taken for granted. After the years go by, it is easy to forget the way things were, and fail to appreciate the blessed difference of Christ in our lives.

There are two kinds of people in this world: those who know Jesus Christ and those who don't. Those who know Him know why they are here and where they are going. They know the richness of God's love and the hope of His glory. They know they are safe concerning the eternal future of their souls. Those who do not know Jesus are either hopeless or deceived. They may be deceived and think that it really does not matter. They may have some answers, and even give their lives in the pursuit of them, but they do not know the joy that is to be had in reconciliation with their Maker.

Those who know Jesus need to be His messengers to those who don't. Now is the day of salvation (2Corinthians 6:2). The Lord is **not willing that any should perish, but that all should come to repentance (2Peter 3:9),** but this day will eventually come to an end. At some point, justice will be administered and it will be severe. Now is the time to take hold of God's gracious provision: **For God so loved the world, that He gave His only begotten Son, that whoever believes in Him should not perish, but have everlasting life (John 3:16).**

Multitudes mistakenly worship false gods due to fear, while *God so loved the world.* But they cannot believe if they do not know.   That's where we come in. Jesus said, **"the gospel must first be preached to all the nations" (Mark 13:10).**   This is our mission. As children of hope, and in view of the end, we are to make it known to the world that Christ died for their sins.

The missionary type

"I'm not the missionary type," you may say, but the truth is that ALL Christians are missionaries. Our number one mission is to **love the Lord your God with all your heart, and with all your soul, and with all your mind (Matthew 22:37).** This mission involves the turning from sin and the **pressing on toward the mark for the prize of the high calling of God in Christ Jesus (Philippians 3:14).**   Then, our mission is to love one another, to **love your neighbor as yourself (Matthew 22:39).** These are the Lord's commands, and our mission is to fulfill them.

David prophesied that **all the ends of the world shall remember and turn unto the LORD: and all the kindreds of the nations shall worship before thee (Psalm 22:27; KJV).** But how will they know if we keep quiet? No matter where we are, we are in the world. That means we have the opportunity to help fulfill this prophecy. Whether in America, China, South Africa, India, or anywhere else, the Christian's mission is to set forth the gospel of Jesus Christ. Every Christian is a missionary, unless they do not mean it when they pray, "Thy Kingdom come, thy will be done."

Not all missionaries are preachers. One does not have to preach in order to be involved in spreading the good news. There are other ways to actively witness for Christ, either at home or abroad. Some might go to the front lines and care for starving children in the inner city, or in India. Some might concentrate more on intercessory prayer or financial support for workers overseas or locally. Others might work behind the scenes for a church or a special ministry. They will see themselves as missionaries, whether they are 'on the field' or in the workplace. Their hearts will be united with the missionary efforts of others within the family of Christ.

Many great Christian leaders have testified of certain individuals who faithfully prayed for their life and work. These kinds of prayer warriors may not send out monthly newsletters or speak at church, but their ministry is vital. No, the question is not whether you are a missionary or not, the question is *what kind of missionary you are.*

Though some believers may not have the gift of speaking, they should not be shy about their life in Christ. This does not mean that an evangelistic presentation is always required; but God can use any sincere testimony, and good works speak volumes. In this world of darkness,

> **You are the light of the world. A city that is set on a hill cannot be hidden. Nor do they light a lamp and put it under a basket, but on a lampstand, and it gives light to all who are in the house. Let your light so shine before men, that they may see your good works and glorify your Father in heaven. (Matthew 5:14-16).**

When a flame is covered, it will go out. Stronger flames will be harder to contain. The more intimate our relationship with Jesus, the less we will be able to keep quiet. We often speak or act according to our hearts' inclinations, so the more Jesus reigns in the heart, the more natural the witness will be.

The idea is to shine. Jesus said, **"I am the light of the world: he that follows me shall not walk in darkness, but have the light of life" (John 8:12).** This light of life is but a foreshadow of the glow that will light up the new Jerusalem, as John prophesied in **Revelation 21:23: "The city had no need of the sun or of the moon to shine in it, for the glory of God illuminated it. The Lamb is its light."** What wondrous light! The sun is bright but the Son is brighter! This is the light we have received.

The needy

Meanwhile, there are people all around us who do not enjoy the same blessing. Some willfully choose to reject it. Some are rebels, grasping for significance in their defiance of authority. Some are pleasure seekers, able to gratify their senses but unable to satisfy their souls. Others are just struggling to survive. They all have passions and longings for abundant life, but their experience often amounts to little more than this:

> **Just exactly as he came, so shall he go. And what profit has he who has labored for the wind? All his days he also eats in darkness, and he has much sorrow and sickness and anger (Ecclesiastes 5:16-17).**

They all have souls. They all need God's love. Made in God's image, they all have loving potential. But death has a present claim on them.

Jesus came to this world to revoke that claim. He **was the true Light, which lighteth every man that cometh into the world... as many as received Him, to them gave He power to become the sons of God, even to them that believe on His name (John 1:9,12; KJV).**

And the offer still exists, **for whoever calls upon the name of the Lord shall be saved (Romans 10:13).** He has chosen you and me to carry this important message! It is a tremendous and significant opportunity that is often carelessly missed. There are some people out there who are just waiting for the good news, though it may appear otherwise.

"I know I would have responded to the gospel a lot sooner," a sister told me, "if someone would have shared it with me. But I was into some weird stuff, and the way I looked probably scared them away."

The Great Commission

The Bible reveals God's heartbeat throughout history to gather His children unto Himself. He intended from the beginning that all nations should be blessed through Abraham (see Genesis 12:3). Jesus came to seek and save the lost. The disciples were commanded to go and make disciples of all nations (Matthew 28:19). The Lamb is destined to receive worship from **a great multitude, which no man [can] number, of all nations, and kindreds, and people, and tongues (Revelation 7:9).** We have the opportunity to join God in His high mission. He will ultimately accomplish His purposes with or without us, but we deprive ourselves and others if we do not get in on the action.

It is the opportunity to help bring about eternal change. It is the opportunity to bless God, to serve Him in this area He deems so important: the reaching of the lost. It is the opportunity to see the Light come into people's lives, and to be used in the process.

* * * * * * *

Christmas is now a big event in China, but in 1999 it was hardly known. As I began to teach my English class there, I drew a picture of Santa Claus on the blackboard. I thought I would lead into the lesson speaking about cultural traditions. "Do you know who this is?" I asked, and received mostly blank stares. One person in the back raised his hand and asked, "Is it Jesus?"

Most of the students hadn't even heard of Jesus, and the few who had didn't have a clue as to who He was. It was a real blessing to be the first to help them understand.

Missions provide opportunities for many blessings, including the joy of seeing people come to know Christ, seeing lives rescued from the darkness, and extending God's Kingdom further on this earth. So much is missed because there is fear of leaving the security of the mundane. It can be difficult to go out on a limb for God, but that is where the fruit of faith hangs. Sometimes it is hard to take first steps, but **without faith it is impossible to please Him, for he who comes to God must believe that He is, and that He is a rewarder of those who diligently seek Him. (Hebrews 11:6).**

Do you feel called to go where the gospel needs to be demonstrated and heard? Why miss out? Is God unable to take care of you? He is a rewarder of them that diligently seek Him. Jesus said that there is no one who has **left house, or parents, or brethren, or wife, or children, for the kingdom of God's sake, who shall not receive manifold more in this present time, and in the world to come life everlasting (Luke 18:29-30; KJV).**

Are you called to stay? You could support those who go. They need help financially, and your praying may be key to the harvest. You can familiarize yourself more with the needs of the area and its people by doing research and reading. Your encouragement can refresh the workers there. You might take care of tasks for them on the home front, or send them things they need overseas. Send them goodies too! Communicate with them and pray for them often.

Wherever you are, you can make a difference. There are opportunities to reach the nations right where you live. There are many international students at local universities. International businesspeople often spend a term in America. Most of these people will return to their homelands. Your witness to them may get carried overseas and affect an entire country.

In America, it is easy to forget that there may be foreigners here who need a welcoming friend. This is because it is a 'melting pot' culture, and hard to recognize who is visiting or who has just arrived. I know of more than one Chinese person who never made any friends when they visited America, and came back to China with a negative impression. Be sensitive to the possibility that the foreigners you see may only be visitors. You could be their only exposure to the gospel, and you might be their only friend.

Somebody may be waiting for your witness. My wife Jennifer was blessed in China while riding a bicycle alongside her new sister in the Lord. This woman had been telling her about how incredible it was that she could actually know God, and also that her previous kidney troubles had disappeared since she had believed. Jennifer started to say, "Maybe the Lord sent me…" and her friend completed the sentence:

"To tell *me* the good news!"

Jesus said to His disciples, **"I also send you" (John 20:21).** You are no ordinary person; you are a child of the Most High God. All of God's children can minister the light of Christ, as they walk in the light as He is in the light. You may not be ordained, but you are commissioned. You may not be perfect, but God uses imperfect people. You may not be strong, but His strength is made perfect in weakness. You may not be wise, but He chooses **the foolish things of the world to put to shame the wise (1Corinthians 1:27).** Do you love God? Do you love the Father, Son, and Holy Spirit? Then you are qualified! Prayerfully consider what kind of missionary you are.

God's work is a royal errand. It is also a royal privilege. So many work for that which will perish, but when Christ appears, **you will receive a crown of glory that does not fade away (1Peter 5:4).**

Lord, open our eyes to these truths and help us to run the race effectively. Reveal your love in such a way that we would count everything else as rubbish. Thank you for the promise that you will draw near to us when we draw near to you (James 4:8). Thank you for the heavenly prize we have in Christ Jesus, for He is worthy of all glory, honor and praise.

Amen.

You can participate in world missions and/or help support
Rick and Jennifer Bell through:

Global Outreach International
P.O. Box 1
Tupelo, MS 38802

662-842-4615
www.globaloutreach.org

STUDY GUIDE

Suggestions:

- Before discussion, ask if anything stood out or made an impression in the chapter.
- Where several verses are listed, (in a group setting) divide them up for different individuals to read.
- If a discussion starts to take off, don't feel bound to the questions. Let there be a free flow...
- On the other hand, if a discussion is going off on a tangent, or a point is being over emphasized, don't be afraid to pull everyone back on track.
- Ask God to give revelation and understanding.

Chapter 1
Amazing Truth

1. What is sin? Define in your own words, and then compare with these passages: 1John 3:4; 1John 3:8; James 4:17; Romans 11:20; and Matthew 5:48.

2. Can you give any examples of how the media (film, television, magazines, etc.) encourages sin?

3. What are the effects of sin on an individual, a group, or a society? Consider Romans 6:23; Ezekiel 18:4; and Proverbs 14:34.

4. Describe the relationship between Jesus and our sins according to these passages: 1 Peter 2:22; 2Corinthians 5:21; John 1:29; and Romans 5:6-8.

5. Read John 4:23-24. What does it mean to worship in spirit and in truth? How do they work together?

6. Complete this statement: "A Christian needs the Holy Spirit because_____."

7. Read Acts 1:4-8. Why did Jesus tell the disciples to wait in Jerusalem until they received the baptism of the Holy Spirit?

8. What does it mean to "count all things loss for the excellency of the knowledge of Christ Jesus"? (Philippians 3:8). How is one able to do this?

9. What is the point behind the example of the McDonald's cheese-burgers and the "pork blubber with goat cheese"?

10. Some people read the Bible every day only because they think it is their "Christian duty." What are some better reasons to read the Bible?

Chapter 2
Fire in the Word

1. The Bible contains 66 different books and has at least 40 different human authors from different places and different times in history. Yet it contains one consistent theme of God's redemption. Can you think of other aspects of the Word that make it a unique book?

2. Read Psalm 119:9-16; Psalm 119:105; 2 Timothy 3:16-17; and Matthew 4:1-11. What do these passages say about the purpose of Scripture and the best way to use it? How might Scripture be misused?

3. As the Bible is no ordinary book, how should it be read (in comparison to reading other books)?

4. Read Titus 3:1-11 and 2Timothy 2:22-26. What are we to affirm and what are we to avoid?

5. In Philippians 2:1-2, what are the four components Paul uses to promote like-mindedness and love, and explain how each of them play a role in the Christian life. Do you see this happening among believers?

6. Read Galatians 5:22-26. How might this passage be used in relation to debates and differences within the Church?

7. Do you think debating is effective? When is it effective, and when is it not?

8. Some tenets of the Christian faith must not be compromised. Which ones? (John 3:16-19; Titus 3:3-8; 1John 5:1; and 2John 9 might be helpful here).

9. Read Luke 18:10-14. The tax collector was considered the lowest of low on the face of the earth! Why was he justified, and not the Pharisee? Who probably knew the Word better?

10. What is the Holy Spirit's role in our understanding of the Word? Consider John 16:13-15. What might be a good prayer to make according to this passage?

Chapter 3
Aliens and Strangers

1. Read John 5:6-14 and John 8:1-11. Discuss how Jesus balanced righteous standards with non-condemning love.

2. Read Matthew 23:25-28 and Matthew 5:1-12. What kind of traits did Jesus speak so strongly against, and what kind did He speak so favorably for?

3. Read John 3:17 and Acts 17:31. Are these two scriptures at odds? How are they reconciled and how might each influence us in our Christian living?

4. What would be an example of meeting non-Christians on their own ground, in contrast to compromising and meeting them in a sinful environment?

5. How do these verses describe the 'carnal' or 'fleshly' Christian? 1Corinthians 3:1-4; 2Corinthians 10:3-5; Romans 8:4-6.

6. Explain the difference between true holiness and self-righteousness.

7. What makes somebody "unholy"? Answer in your own words and then compare with Matthew 15:1-20.

8. What makes believers holy, according to Acts 10:13-15; Hebrews 10:14; Hebrews 7:19; and Hebrews 9:14?

9. Read John 13:5-10. How is it that we are clean and why do we need "our feet" washed?

10. What are the keys to gladness as suggested in this chapter?

Chapter 4
Loosen Up

1. In your own words, what is sanctification? Discuss what the following verses reveal about sanctification: Exodus 13:2 Exodus 29:44 Leviticus 10:10 Leviticus 11: 44-45   Numbers 3:12   Isaiah 1:16-17 Ezekiel 36:25-26 Mark 3:35   John 17:19 Ephesians 4:1   Colossians 3:1-4 1Thessalonians 4:3-4, 7

2. Read Romans 6:1-18. Which verses speak of knowing and believing and which verses speak of actions or doing? How do they relate to each other?

3. What specific things are we to know and believe in these verses?

4. How might you explain the contrast between Romans 6:11, being "dead to sin" with Romans 7:14, being "sold unto sin"?

5. Explain the importance and role of the mind in Christian living, according to Romans 12:1-2.

6. What is unbelief? Can unbelief co-exist with faith? How? See Mark 9:24.

7. What can be done to reduce unbelief in a Christian's life? Consider Matthew 17:20-21 and Ephesians 4:17-24.

8. Read Ezekiel 36:22-30. Explain God's purposes and methods of sanctification according to this passage. How might it apply to us as the church today?

9. Should holy living be difficult? Consider Matthew 11:30; 1John 5:3; and 2Timothy 3:12.

10. Your friend says that he or she is a Christian, but really seems to care less about living a holy life. If you could say something to him or her, what would it be?

Chapter 5
The Truth About Death

1. What are the consequences of Adam's sin, according to Genesis 2:16-17; Genesis 3:17-19; Romans 5:12; and Ezekiel 18:4 ?

2. Read Romans 5:15-19 and 1Corinthians 15:13-22. According to these passages, what did we receive from Adam and what did we receive from Jesus?

3. In your own words, what is eternal life? Discuss how it is depicted in these passages: John 17:3; John 10:10; Revelation 21:4; and Revelation 22:1-5.

4. "What goes down must come up." Explain this statement in terms of trusting or following the Lord on a daily basis. Use these verses to help: 1 Peter 5:6; Matthew 23:12; and Luke 14:8-10.

5. What does taking up the cross mean to you? Does every trial in life count as a cross to bear?

6. How does God use suffering? Does all that happens come directly from Him?   Consider Genesis 50:20; Lamentations 3:33; Isaiah 54:15; Jeremiah 19:5; Luke 13:1-5; and Acts 2:23.

7. Can you share of a time when you suffered and later saw good come from it?

8. Read Philippians 1:21-25; Acts 20:22-24; and 2Timothy 4:6-8. Discuss Paul's view of dying, and what it was that motivated him.

9. Read Romans 12:9-21. Where does denying the self play a role in these verses?

10. Is there some tendency or habit in your life that you would like to see die? Is it up to God or up to you?

Chapter 6
Peace and Glory

1. Can you describe a time that you were in a tough situation and yet had a peace that helped you through?

2. Read Isaiah 43:1-2; Psalm 91:15; and 2Timothy 4:17-18 . What can we expect from God in fearful situations?

3. Read Psalm 121. Does this mean that bad things will never happen?   How can you use this Psalm in a trial?   What do you find most comforting about it?

4. Explain the concept of faith as an issue of having certainty vs. just knowing Who to go to. Consider Hebrews 11:1; 1Peter 1:8; Psalm 27:13; Psalm 42:11; and Romans 4:19-22.

5. In Jesus, sin is no longer counted against believers. Does this mean it is okay to sin? Consider Romans 6; Galatians 5:13; 1Peter 2:16; 2Peter 2:19-22; and Jude 4.

6. Consider a sin, like adultery for example. Though a Christian may be forgiven, he or she is not free from the consequences that result. Brainstorm and think of all the damage and destruction that can result from such a sin. Consider who it effects besides the immediate perpetrators. How about hypocrisy or lying? Drunkenness? Bitterness?

7. Give testimony of a conviction that came in your life, and the change that resulted.

8. What do you think is glorious in this world? How do these passages describe God's glory: Romans 8:18; 2Corinthians 4:16-18; and 1Corinthians 2:9 ?

9. How does God presently manifest His glory on earth, according to: Psalm 8:3; Psalm 145:10; Romans 15:9; 1Corinthians 6:20; 2Corinthians 9:10-13; and 1Peter 2:12 ?

10. How will God be glorified in time to come, according to: Isaiah 40:5; Habakkuk 2:14; Psalm 86:9; Daniel 7:14,27; Romans 11:11-15, 23-25; Revelation 11:15; and Revelation 21:23-24 ?

Chapter 7
Peace and Love

1.   Can you give examples of faulty characterizations of love in the media? Any examples of good characterizations of love?

2. 1Corinthians 13 is the "great love chapter" in the Bible. Can you remember or guess what specific characteristics of love are listed there? Discuss and then check your answers.

3. What does 1Corinthians 13 tell us about ourselves? The church?

4. Read 1John 4:7-21. How is God's love manifested to us? What are the effects of His love upon us, according to this passage?

5. What is perfect love and how does perfect love cast out fear (1John 4:17-18)?

6. What is the difference between knowing and believing God's love (1John 4:16)?

7. Read Romans 8:31-39. Find and describe the different acts and expressions of love.

8. You continually receive rude treatment from a co-worker, class-mate, neighbor, or family member. What will you do? Consider Romans 12:17-21; 1Peter 2:18-21; 2Samuel 16:5-12; Isaiah 54:15-17; and Luke 6:35.

9. Should love just put up with everything? Check your answer with Proverbs 27:6;   Psalm 141:5;   Mark 11:15-17; and Revelation 3:19.

10. How can your study group spur one another on to love and good works (Hebrews 10:24)?

Chapter 8
Peace and Quiet

1. Share a special time that God answered a prayer for you.

2. Should we expect answers to prayer in our day on the same level with those in Bible times? Consider James 5:13-18; Hebrews 13:8; and John 14:12.

3. What's wrong with this prayer? "Lord, if you want to, please make me filthy rich!" Check James 4:3 and 3John 2.

4. Read Daniel 9:20-23, and then Daniel 10:10-13. In each case, when was Daniel's prayer answered and how long did it take for him to realize it? What does this teach us about prayer?

5. Why have a daily quiet time?

6. Read Paul's prayer in Ephesians 1:15-23. Does Paul ask for hope, glory and power for the church, or does he assume it is already given? What specifically does he ask for?

7. "God please be with us now." According to Hebrews 13:5 and Matthew 18:20, is this a faithful prayer? If not, how could you turn it into one?

8. The Psalms are an excellent place to learn how to pray. Yet some Old Testament prayers do not fit within a New Testament context (Psalm 109, for example): the cross changed our situation. Read Psalm 51:10-11. Would these verses be a faithful prayer within the position of the New Covenant and these passages: Hebrews 8:10-13; 2Peter 1:9; Hebrews 13:5; Ephesians 1:13; and Ephesians 4:30 ?

9. Compare Psalm 42:2 with John 6:35. Which verse do you relate to more? How does Psalm 42:4-6, 8, and 11 offer helpful instruction for feelings of emptiness or despair? Look also at James 4:8.

10. Does praying in faith mean that you do nothing else? When should we act and when shouldn't we? Consider James 2:17-20; Matthew 9:20-22; Genesis 16:1-4; and Galatians 4:22-31.

Chapter 9
Hope in the Middle of it All

1. Read Ecclesiastes 1:1-11; 6:12; 7:15; 8:10-15; 12:13-14. What is the point Solomon is trying to make? Is he speaking of life in consideration of the gospel?

2. Read Proverbs 23:17-18; 1Thessalonians 5:1-11; and 1John 3:2-3. How can gospel hope help a believer to resist temptation?

3. Read Romans 5:3-5; Romans 8:18; 2Corinthians 4:16-5:1; and 1Peter 3:12-15.   How can gospel hope help assist a believer in times of suffering?

4. How might hope help you when your faith is disappointed? Consider Hebrews 11:13-16 and Romans 8:28

5. What is the hopeful outcome of a trial of faith, according to 1Peter 1:3-9 and James 1:2-4?

6. Contrast the hope of Jesus Christ with the hope of the Old Covenant law, considering Hebrews 7:19;   Romans 3:19-26;   Romans 6:14; Galatians 3:10; and Galatians 4:3-7.

7. What is the hope of your progress and spiritual growth when you feel you are making no progress? See Psalm 138:8 and Philippians 1:6.

8. What can you do to build up hope in your life?

9. Different groups in the church interpret Christ's return in widely different ways. What do you think is most important to keep in mind? Should believers spend a lot of time trying to figure all the details out?

10. According to Matthew 24:14, when will the end come?

Chapter 10
Jesus is the Light of the World

1. You may or may not be called to go overseas. But if there were any place you would go as a missionary, where would it be, and why?

2. Why is prayer alone insufficient for winning the lost to Christ? Consider Romans 10:13-17.

3. What are the primary goals of missions, according to these passages: Matthew 28:19-20;   Luke 24:46-47;   Psalm 22:27-28;   James 1:27; Isaiah 58:6-7; Galatians 6:9-10; 1John 3:16-18; Mark 16:16-15; and Philippians 2:9-11?

4. What was the gospel as proclaimed by Jesus?   Check Matthew 4:17; Mark 1:14-15; Mark 6:12;   Luke 4:18-19;   Luke 4:43;   Luke 8:1; and Luke 24:47.

5. What was the gospel as proclaimed by the apostles? Check Acts 2:38; Acts 3:19-21; Acts 4:1-2, 33;   Acts 17:18;   Acts 23:6;   Acts 26:20; Acts 10:42-43;   Romans 10:9-13; and Romans 6:23.

6. What is the gospel as proclaimed by the church in our day?

7. The Pharisees were adamant missionaries (Matt.23:15). How can we avoid being like them in missions?   Consider Galatians 5:6 and 1Corinthians 13:3.

8. Have you ever been turned off or ashamed by a missionary effort? What could have been done differently?

9. In just a few sentences, how did you come to know the Lord? What changed in your life?

10. What can you and/or this group do to participate in the missionary work of Jesus Christ?